Educator Wellness

A Guide for Sustaining **Physical**, **Mental**, **Emotional**, and **Social** Well-Being

Timothy D. Kanold
Tina H. Boogren

Solution Tree | Press

a division of
Solution Tree

555 North Morton Street
Bloomington, IN 47404
800.733.6786 (toll free) / 812.336.7700
FAX: 812.336.7790

email: info@SolutionTree.com
SolutionTree.com

Visit **go.SolutionTree.com/educatorwellness** to download the free reproducibles in this book.

Printed in the United States of America

Library of Congress Cataloging-in-Publication Data

Names: Kanold, Timothy D., author. | Boogren, Tina, author.
Title: Educator wellness : a guide for sustaining physical, mental,
  emotional, and social well-being / Timothy D. Kanold, Tina H. Boogren.
Description: Bloomington : Solution Tree Press, [2021] | Includes
  bibliographical references and index.
Identifiers: LCCN 2021035550 (print) | LCCN 2021035551 (ebook) | ISBN
  9781954631090 (paperback) | ISBN 9781954631106 (ebook)
Subjects: LCSH: Teachers--Mental health. | Physical education and training.
  | Emotional intelligence. | Teachers--Social conditions. | Reflective
  teaching.
Classification: LCC LB2840 .K34 2021 (print) | LCC LB2840 (ebook) | DDC
  371.102--dc23
LC record available at https://lccn.loc.gov/2021035550
LC ebook record available at https://lccn.loc.gov/2021035551

Solution Tree
Jeffrey C. Jones, CEO
Edmund M. Ackerman, President

Solution Tree Press
President and Publisher: Douglas M. Rife
Associate Publisher: Sarah Payne-Mills
Managing Production Editor: Kendra Slayton
Editorial Director: Todd Brakke
Art Director: Rian Anderson
Copy Chief: Jessi Finn
Senior Production Editor: Tonya Maddox Cupp
Content Development Specialist: Amy Rubenstein
Copy Editor: Mark Hain
Proofreader: Sarah Ludwig
Text and Cover Designer: Rian Anderson
Editorial Assistants: Sarah Ludwig and Elijah Oates

To Susan. You have modeled for me, and taught me how to respect and care for my wellness, in order to do the same for others. Thank you for choosing to build the path of your life, with me.

—Timothy D. Kanold

This book is dedicated to my husband, Eric. Having you as my partner in all things helps me live my best life and for that, I am forever grateful.

—Tina H. Boogren

Acknowledgments

The concept for this *Educator Wellness* book and project was birthed by our individual, and then our collaborative, response to the relentless stress and change placed on every educator who navigates our incredible profession.

When we presented the concept of Wellness Solutions for Educators™ to Jeff Jones and the leaders at Solution Tree, they immediately embraced the idea and, more important, helped advance, improve, and launch our concept into a reality. We cannot thank Douglas Rife, Sarah Payne-Mills, Shannon Ritz, Ali Cummins, Renee Marshall, Claudia Wheatley, Jesse Loudenbarger, and Erica Dooley-Dorocke enough. Special thanks to Jeff Jones as well, whose belief in supporting the work of the authors is only surpassed by his actions.

A book like this requires an unending amount of time, drafts and re-writes, and more. If it reads well, it is only because of the lead editor and her editorial team. Special thanks to Tonya Cupp, who cares about this topic as much as we do, and who gave so much of her own time and wisdom to make the book so much more fluid and complete for you, the reader. Thanks, too, to Sarah, Rian, Amy, Mark, and Elijah from her team!

We would also like to thank our reviewers extraordinaire: Chris Mason, Julie Schmidt, Jeremy Adams, Jessica Hannigan, Jasmine Kullar, Paula Maeker, Joshua Ray, Georgina Rivera, Nathan Lang-Raad, Angie Freese, Katie Graves, Amy Kozucko, and Annie Woofley. Each brought special insight, wisdom, and perspective to us about the topics of wellness and educator care. We are in their debt for making the book and its fundamental dimensions and routines stronger in its research and in its communication to you.

Special thanks go to superintendent Janel Keating and her faculty and staff in White River School District (Washington state) for their feedback to our rating and reflecting protocols. Similar thanks go to assistant superintendent Jeanne Spiller and her staff in Kildeer Countryside School District (Illinois). Your collective feedback effort has helped us improve our work from the practitioner's point of view.

Finally, we want to thank you for taking the time to pick up this book, read and write your way through it, and giving yourself the gift of wellness through your personal self-care and self-compassion. It is true—our profession has its challenging moments and exhausting days. It also has the incredible opportunity to impact the lives of so many. To overcome that exhaustion and experience the joy of that impact requires an intentional examination and a positive daily response to our health and well-being.

May this book, with its four dimensions of wellness, and its twelve routines for improvement, help you live your best life, every day!

Tim Kanold and Tina Boogren

Visit **go.SolutionTree.com/educatorwellness** to download the free reproducibles in this book.

Table of Contents

About the Authors

 **Timothy D. Kanold, PhD,** is an award-winning educator and author. He is former director of mathematics and science and served as superintendent of Adlai E. Stevenson High School District 125, a model professional learning community (PLC) district in Lincolnshire, Illinois.

Dr. Kanold has authored or coauthored more than thirty textbooks and books on K–12 mathematics, school culture, and school leadership, including his best-selling and 2018 Independent Publisher Book Award-winning book *HEART! Fully Forming Your Professional Life as a Teacher and Leader*. He has most recently authored a sequel to *HEART!*, the book *SOUL! Fulfilling the Promise of Your Professional Life as a Teacher and Leader*.

Dr. Kanold received the 2017 Ross Taylor / Glenn Gilbert National Leadership Award from the National Council of Supervisors of Mathematics, the international 2010 Damen Award for outstanding contributions to education from Loyola University Chicago, and the 1986 Presidential Award for Excellence in Mathematics and Science Teaching.

Dr. Kanold earned a bachelor's degree in education and a master's degree in applied mathematics from Illinois State University. He received his doctorate in educational leadership and counseling psychology from Loyola University Chicago.

Dr. Kanold is committed to equity, excellence, and social justice reform for the improved learning of students and school faculty, staff, and administrators. He conducts inspirational professional development seminars worldwide with a focus on improving student learning outcomes through a commitment to the PLC process and a focus on living a well-balanced, fully engaged professional life by practicing reflection and self-care routines.

To learn more about Dr. Kanold's work, follow him @tkanold, #heartandsoul4ED, or #liveyourbestlife on Twitter.

Tina H. Boogren, PhD, is a fierce advocate for educators and an award-winning educator, best-selling author, and highly sought-after speaker. She has proudly served as a classroom teacher, mentor, instructional coach, and building-level leader and has presented for audiences all over the world.

Dr. Boogren is deeply committed to supporting educators so that they can support their students. She conducts highly requested and inspiring keynotes, workshops, and virtual webinars that focus on quality instruction, coaching, mentoring, and educator wellness, and she hosts a weekly podcast, *Self-Care for Educators with Dr. Tina H. Boogren.*

Dr. Boogren was a 2007 finalist for Colorado Teacher of the Year and was a recipient of her school district's Outstanding Teacher Award eight years in a row, from 2002 to 2009. She is the author of numerous books, including *In the First Few Years: Reflections of a Beginning Teacher, Supporting Beginning Teachers, The Beginning Teacher's Field Guide: Embarking on Your First Years, 180 Days of Self-Care for Busy Educators, Take Time for You: Self-Care Action Plans for Educators,* which was the Independent Publisher Book Award gold winner in the education category, and *Coaching for Educator Wellness: A Guide to Supporting New and Experienced Teachers.* She is a coauthor of *Motivating and Inspiring Students: Strategies to Awaken the Learner* along with Robert J. Marzano, Darrell Scott, and Ming Lee Newcomb, and is a contributing author to Richard Kellough's *Middle School Teaching: A Guide to Methods and Resources* and Robert J. Marzano's *Becoming a Reflective Teacher.*

Dr. Boogren holds a bachelor's degree from the University of Iowa, a master's degree with an administrative endorsement from the University of Colorado Denver, and a doctorate from the University of Denver in educational administration and policy studies.

To learn more about Dr. Boogren's work, follow her at #THBoogren or #liveyourbestlife on Twitter or at @TinaHBoogren on Facebook, join her Facebook group (www.facebook.com/selfcareforeducators), and listen to her podcast, *Self-Care for Educators with Dr. Tina H. Boogren* (www.selfcareforeducators.com).

Introduction

We are a profession of *physical, mental, emotional, and social labor.*

Would you agree?

As educators, every day, we are immersed in our social experiences and our common humanity with many others—our colleagues, our students, and often the families of our students. And that immersion can take its toll on our physical, mental, emotional, and social well-being. We are whole, complex, emotion-filled teachers, administrators, instructional coaches, counselors, social workers, nurses, support staff, and more. As such, we make thousands of decisions every week, we experience a wide array of emotions from our students and colleagues, we adapt and change, and if we are not careful, it can leave us in a state of prolonged stress.

Emotional exhaustion, loneliness, and burnout lurk in the doorways of our classrooms and office spaces. We hold the razor-thin line between exhaustion and joy in the palm of our hands, every day.

Which brings us, Tim Kanold and Tina Boogren, to why we wrote this guidebook for educator wellness. Think of your health as representing your state of well-being. Then, think of wellness as an action that enhances your state of well-being.

Thus, for the purposes of this guidebook, we define *educator wellness* as *a continuous, active process toward achieving a positive state of good health and enhanced physical, mental, emotional, and social well-being.*

Notice in the definition, educator wellness is not a singular event. It is a *process* of self-reflecting routines for a lifetime of continuous growth and improvement—every day, every month, every season, every school year. In a sense, it is a lifestyle of pursuing improved habits and routines. There will be growth, and setbacks, and more growth again as we determine how to initiate and then sustain helpful wellness routines into our professional lives.

Does your wellness as an education professional really matter? It does. Your well-being matters first and foremost to you, as you are the primary beneficiary of living your best life as an educator.

Your well-being matters to your students and colleagues as they become the beneficiaries of your improved energy and engagement, your efficient and wise daily decision making, your sense of self-efficacy, and your commitment to balancing a busy life with routines that allow your brain to process thousands of inputs from each day. Your students and colleagues benefit from your avoidance of prolonged stress and your wise decisions to listen without judgment.

This wellness guidebook is written for every educator. Every one of us who has chosen a role in this profession. As you read the guidebook, sometimes we use the term *educator* and sometimes we use the phrase *teacher and leader*. We use these terms interchangeably to represent every adult role in the school enterprise, including paraprofessionals, counselors, social workers, tutors, and support staff—as directly or indirectly, we are all teachers and leaders of our students and our colleagues.

Also note we—Tim and Tina—often use the words *we* and *our*. In most cases, we are referring to ourselves as the authors of the book, and are living these same wellness routines right beside you! At other times, *we (Tim and Tina)* will make a distinction that it is our voice talking more directly to you, as a reader.

Thus, *we* present four core dimensions of professional wellness.

1. Physical
2. Mental
3. Emotional
4. Social

Each dimension has three specific corresponding wellness routines designed to support and focus your efforts toward improving your professional life.

The first three chapters of this guidebook represent our (1) physical, (2) mental, and (3) emotional wellness dimensions. These dimensions tend to be more personal and self-regulatory—you own your personal improvement. The fourth chapter, however, is about your social wellness dimension and brings together the relational benefits to your students and colleagues from your effort and actions described in chapters 1 through 3. Appendix A offers the Wellness Solutions for

Educators™ framework; appendix B provides a protocol for rating, reflecting, goal setting, planning, and progress monitoring; and appendix C provides a self-evaluation rubric.

These three tools provide twelve routines for you and your colleagues to consider as you reflect on your personal or collective wellness plan progress, create meaningful and focused short-term and long-term professional wellness goals, and take action to achieve those goals.

As you read and journal through this research-affirmed guidebook, know that improving your routines in each of these wellness dimensions can have an exponential impact on the quality of your work and life. The whole is greater than the sum of its parts. Figure I.1 provides a graphic model for the Wellness Solutions for Educators framework.

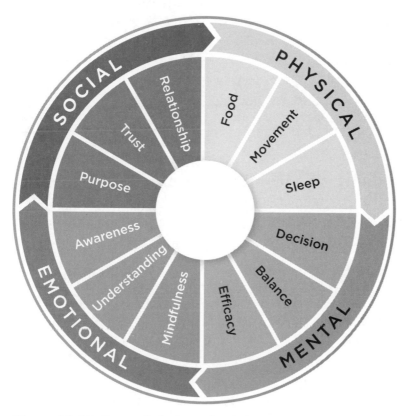

Figure I.1: Wellness Solutions for Educators framework graphic model.

Chapter 1: The Physical Wellness Dimension

Our lives as educators thrive and flourish when we reflect on and improve routines for physical wellness. The physical wellness dimension is based on our most foundational needs and asks us to measure our progress on three distinct physical wellness routines.

1. **Food routines:** Consider what and when you eat and drink, and how well you hydrate during the day.

2. **Movement routines:** Consider what, when, and how well you move during the day.

3. **Sleep routines:** Consider how much sleep *and* rest you get during each twenty-four-hour cycle.

This chapter brings into focus how well you take care of yourself physically, as your first and primary need as an educator. You will take a deep dive into how these three routines are interconnected. In general, improving one area of your food, movement, and sleep routines is a great start, yet may not be sufficient since these three routines are interdependent on one another. However, focused improvement in all three routines has benefits for every aspect of your wellness as an educator.

Chapter 2: The Mental Wellness Dimension

Our lives as educators also thrive as we improve our routines for mental wellness. This mental wellness dimension is based on our need to live busy and highly engaged lives with stress levels that are good for us, while avoiding the crossover into a daily, hurried, out-of-control, prolonged stress work life. The mental wellness dimension is based on our time, energy, decision-making, balance, and confidence needs and asks us to measure our progress on three distinct wellness routines.

1. **Decision routines:** Consider how well you reduce, automate, and regulate the decisions you make each day to avoid decision fatigue.

2. **Balance routines:** Consider how well you live a busy, high-energy, well-balanced day-to-day work life and avoid prolonged stress.

3. **Efficacy routines:** Consider how well you build your confidence and competence and improve your work-life capabilities each day.

This chapter will ask you to reduce the decision-making noise of your busy work and home life and consider how to develop your confidence with just enough humility to know there is still a lot to learn.

Chapter 3: The Emotional Wellness Dimension

Our lives as educators need us to improve our routines for emotional wellness. Recommendations for the routines in this dimension are based on the need for healthy emotional responses to our daily experiences. We measure our progress on three distinct emotional wellness routines.

1. **Awareness routines:** Consider how well you identify, keep track of, and respond to your daily emotions.

2. **Understanding routines:** Consider the why behind your emotions and how well you reflect on your responses to different emotions.

3. **Mindfulness routines:** Consider how well you use mindfulness practices to respond rather than react to your strong and more unpleasant emotions.

This chapter will ask you to consider how you become more aware of your emotions, how written reflection can support your understanding of your emotional state, and how your mindfulness routines result in healthy emotional regulation.

Chapter 4: The Social Wellness Dimension

Our lives as educators begin to expand when we reflect on and improve routines for our social wellness. This practice is based on our need for healthy relationships with students and colleagues as we measure our progress on three distinct social wellness routines.

1. **Relationship routines:** Consider how well you and your colleagues build strong relationships and social connections together.

2. **Trust routines:** Consider how well you build daily work-life routines of vulnerability and deep listening without judgment of others.

3. **Purpose routines:** Consider how your daily work life feeds into your greater purpose and helps you find meaning and joy in your work life.

This chapter will ask you to consider your why. Why did you join this profession? You will also explore the nature of healthy relationships and the practice of listening without judgment. And you will examine several key actions to successful trust building.

Each chapter begins with a brief picture of what the dimension is about, followed by detailed ideas for each routine. Think of this guidebook as a journal for your professional wellness and write your reflections directly into the guidebook. Spaces in the margins are provided for this purpose.

As you use this wellness guidebook, you can keep your responses as a private journal if you wish. You can also consider sharing your reflections with a trusted friend—would that person confirm your self-evaluation? You can also complete the reflection questions as a team activity or as part of a book study, if it is safe and appropriate to do so.

Also, you will notice a section toward the end of each chapter in which we (Tina and Tim) speak directly to you about our stories, our experiences, with each dimension over the years. We then follow up with an opportunity for you to reflect on your previous and current progress for each routine and ask you to plan forward as you write about your own story and your personal and professional experiences with each of these four wellness dimensions. You can use the margins of this book to write or directly respond to the My Wellness Action prompts provided to help you write about your own story.

For each wellness dimension, we provide research-affirmed sources for supporting and enhancing your professional well-being in the service of student learning. Keep your phone handy while you read to scan the QR codes that link to videos of us, Tina and Tim, talking about each wellness dimension. Follow these directions to access the videos if you've not used a QR code before.

1. Open your smartphone camera.

2. Aim your phone's camera at the QR code (but don't actually photograph it). The camera will show tiny yellow brackets around the corners, and a pop-up will prompt you to "Open in YouTube [or Google, or similar]."

3. Tap the prompt to go directly to the video.

Introduction
www.SolutionTree.com/EducatorWellnessIntroduction

You can see our introductory video if you scan the accompanying QR code.

Our ideal outcome is to help you, your team, your school, or your district live your best life so that you can, in turn, meet the daily expectations and needs of your students and colleagues.

We do not believe your professional wellness lives in a vacuum separated from your personal wellness. We understand that many of the educator wellness routines we present in this guidebook have the potential to support many aspects of your personal life as well. However, our lives as educators—much like others in helping professions, such as medical professionals—have a greater burden, gift, and responsibility to bring our best selves to work each day. As medical doctors Ann E. Burke and Patricia J. Hicks indicate, "Maintaining high standards for professional behavior, even under times of stress, is a responsibility that we share for ourselves and our colleagues."[1]

We (Tim and Tina) recognize our guidebook may not be sufficient if you are in acute distress or need immediate help. A guidebook cannot provide the kind of support you may need. Please seek help, support, and advice from a health professional if you have concerns about your overall health and well-being.

We understand wellness is a personal journey of self-reflection, habits, and routines for a lifetime of continuous improvement. Every educator has a wellness story to tell and a wellness story to write. Wellness experiences ebb and flow based on work and life circumstances and decisions. The questions become, How do I bring my best self to my students and colleagues each day?, How do I avoid the mental and emotional exhaustion that waits for me in every school season?, and Which habits and routines have the greatest impact on my wellness as an educator?

So, think of this book as a guidebook toward answering your professional wellness journey questions. Like all journeys, it is not always smooth; there are starts and stops, and obstacles and adversity, and yet, you look back and you can see your progress. You can see and feel the hope. You use what you learn to plan ahead and move forward. It is, after all, your own personal story, in which your professional life resides.

So, join us, and let's take our educator wellness journey together!

CHAPTER 1

The Physical Wellness Dimension

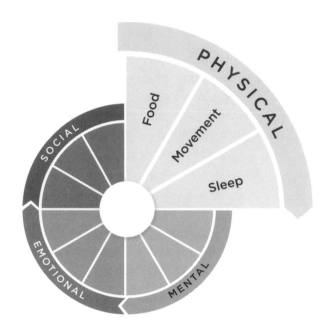

Willpower is about being able to hold opposites. So I can feel the emotion, I can feel the craving, and at the very same time, I just make my awareness big enough to hold my commitment to make a different choice.

— Kelly McGonigal

When we feel better, we are better.

And thus, the first dimension of educator wellness is our physical wellness. Physical wellness includes the core interconnected routines of food, movement, and sleep. When we're eating foods that provide healthy energy to us, we are able to move our bodies more, and when we move our bodies more, we typically sleep better.[2]

Conversely, when we're not eating healthy foods that allow us to feel good, we don't have the desire to move our bodies and we're either unable to sleep or sleep too much.

Physical wellness is essential because our bodies need to be healthy in order to do all the amazing things we want to do—especially serving as effective educators in the service of student learning. Our jobs are not sedentary; they require us to be active. We're up teaching and moving around the classroom and crouching down to work with students on the floor, or we're hustling from one classroom or meeting to another. We are able to meet and match our students' energy levels by taking care of our physical health and the most essential aspects of our overall well-being.

How we care for ourselves physically matters. In fact, it matters *immensely.* How well our bodies function directly impacts our ability to accomplish our daily work tasks as educators and serves as the foundation for the other three wellness dimensions described in this guidebook: our mental, emotional, and social well-being. By first establishing healthy habits and routines for our physical wellness, we create a solid foundation on which to stand and build our overall educator wellness.

The physical wellness dimension of the Wellness Solutions for Educators framework (appendix A, page 81) brings into focus our daily food, movement, and sleep routines. The physical wellness dimension helps us be fully present and engaged in a state of high positive energy for our students and colleagues each day. When we exist in a state of high positive energy, we do our best work. In this energy state, we're more vibrant, enthusiastic, joyful, confident, and fearless. When we pursue a low-positive-energy state, we are more relaxed, tranquil, peaceful, and calm. This is an ideal state for reflection and provides a good balance to our high-positive-energy state expectations.[3]

Consider moments when you've struggled to sustain positive habits in any one of your food, movement, or sleep routines. How did you feel and engage with others? Were you a different person to be around than when you've rocked these routines? Most likely, the answer is yes. When you pay attention to the food you eat, how you move your body, and how much quality sleep you get, you keep your body working properly. And when our bodies are working properly, we are more likely to feel good about the pace of our lives. There is absolutely nothing selfish about taking care of ourselves in these areas.

When we are more balanced, we are busy, but not *hurried*, or stressed. When we are hurried, we feel overwhelmed or stressed by too much to do in too little time. That state of hurry impacts the choices we make around food, movement, and sleep. Consider that our physical wellness tends to be hit the hardest in times of stress and thus, a downward spiral can begin.

For example, ask yourself if you ever sacrifice sleep in order to get your grading done. Do you ever skip lunch so you can cross a few things off your never-ending to-do lists? Do you ever avoid the gym or a doctor (again) because you're just too exhausted to even consider working out or taking time for a routine checkup or minor ailment?

Consider how tightly these three physical wellness routines are interconnected. If we don't get enough sleep, our bodies crave copious amounts of caffeine and sugar, which consuming sends us into a blood sugar spiral, leaving us wired but tired, and then completely fried at the end of the day.[4]

Or, we skip breakfast and lunch and find ourselves ravenous by the time we get home, stuffing processed food in our mouths without even sitting down, leaving us with a stomachache and unable to fall asleep. It's a difficult negative cycle but one that we can absolutely begin to gain control over, starting one step at a time.

Working to improve any of these routines in isolation from the others will not be sustainable or sufficient. We need to work to stabilize each of these areas. Consider how eating the right foods provides energy for workouts and improves the quality of our sleep. Think about how a sound night of sleep increases the likelihood our food choices will support our wellness goals the next day. Research shows that "people who are sleep deprived are more drawn towards high-calorie foods."[5]

When we eat in a way that supports our goals, when we move more, and when we sleep better, we are the primary beneficiaries of the effort—but our students and colleagues benefit as well. Feeling better helps us have a more positive outlook on life and toward people around us and gives us the energy to fully engage with them.

Let's take a closer look at the three interconnected routines associated with physical wellness and why they matter.

Food Routines

Eating well is fundamental to our good health and overall well-being. In this guidebook, we do not advocate for a certain *way* of eating or a specific diet. Instead, our aim is to help you reflect on your current food choices and how the decisions about what you eat or drink make you feel as you strive for overall good nutrition and how they make you feel as you strive to move more and sleep better.

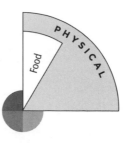

According to the Centers for Disease Control and Prevention (CDC), a healthy eating plan includes a variety of healthy foods. They recommend that you:

> Add an array of colors to your plate and think of it as eating the rainbow. Dark, leafy greens, oranges, and tomatoes—even fresh herbs—are loaded with vitamins, fiber, and minerals. Adding frozen peppers, broccoli, or onions to stews and omelets give them a quick and convenient boost of color and nutrients.[6]

Additionally, good nutrition can reduce the risk of some diseases, lower blood pressure and cholesterol, improve well-being, boost the immune system, and increase energy levels.[7]

When it comes to food, we invite you to consider *what* you eat and drink *and* how your choices make you feel. The *quality* of what we eat is far more important than the *quantity*. Identify the healthiest elements of the foods you like to eat and build them into your lifestyle for the long term. In general, according to a 2020 article in *Medical News Today*, "A healthful diet typically includes nutrient-dense foods from all major food groups, including lean proteins, whole grains, healthful fats, and fruits and vegetables of many colors."[8]

In his best-selling book *Eat Move Sleep*, author Tom Rath reminds us to focus on healthy foods that are good for our short-term energy and serve our long-term health.[9] Additionally, take care to avoid highly processed foods as much as possible. These types of foods include foods like potato chips, cookies, and cereal. It can be easier and more convenient to reach for food in a package, but the adverse health effects of highly processed foods include increased cancer risk; far too much sugar, sodium, and fat; little nutritional value; overindulgence; and artificial ingredients.[10]

Instead, aim to keep your food ingredients simple, shop the outside aisles of your grocery store (where the freshest ingredients are), and cook more meals at home so you can take leftovers to school for lunch the following day.

When it comes to food, we also invite you to consider *how* and *when* you eat and drink. We should feel pleasantly satisfied rather than still ravenous or uncomfortably stuffed after eating. Our food choices should energize us, and that includes being well hydrated throughout the day.

Pay attention to how much water you consume and how staying hydrated helps you feel more energized. An easy way to monitor your hydration is to pay attention to the color of your urine. If your urine is dark and has a strong odor, that's a sure sign of dehydration.[11] Allow yourself adequate time to eat during the school day, without attempting to multitask or being consumed by distractions (like the phone). We should be aware of how our food choices (based on our current eating routines) and the time of day for those food choices impact our mood. Because our meal times are often dictated by the school bell schedule, it may be necessary to plan ahead for a healthy, easy snack such as a piece of fruit or a handful of nuts.

Consider teaming up with your colleagues for additional support. It can be extremely helpful to embark on this journey with others. According to the CDC, working out with a friend provides major benefits, including the following: increased motivation, a willingness to try new things, and consistency.[12] Consider how you can support and respect one another's food choices and needs as well, and how you can make time and create rituals around eating together. You can celebrate short-term wins with goal-supporting food (or a nonfood reward) as you offer both support and respect toward one another's personal food and hydration goals.

According to neurosurgeon and Emory University professor Sanjay Gupta, you can use the acronym S.H.A.R.P. to focus your food routines.[13]

S Slash the sugar
H Hydrate smartly
A Add more omega-3s from natural sources like cold-water fish
R Reduce portions
P Plan meals ahead

Dedicate between three to five days to keeping track of your food and drink routines. Use the data prompts provided in the My Wellness Action section, a digital downloadable tracker (go to https://bit.ly/3sk gvbt), or your own method for tracking the data. As you gather the data, observe your eating and drinking choices, and think about

MY WELLNESS ACTION

Describe patterns observed from your eating and drinking reflections and discoveries. What changes will you make around your food and drink choices next week, based on your reflections from this past week?

You can use this chart to track your eating and hydrating data over three to five days.

Time	What I ate or drank	Where I ate or drank	When I drank water	Context (such as dinner with family)

Gupta's S.H.A.R.P. advice.[14] Be sure to also describe how you felt before, during, and after each meal, snack, and drink.

Movement Routines

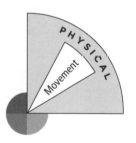

In *Start Here: Master the Lifelong Habit of Wellbeing*, authors Eric Langshur and Nate Klemp state that scientific evidence points to all of the following incredible benefits of movement: enhanced learning, greater productivity, increased resilience to stress, improved mood, and slowed aging.[15] Wow, right? Kelly McGonigal, author of *The Joy of Movement*, adds that movement also activates feelings of pleasure and helps stave off depression.[16] These are all incredible benefits to our educator lives!

When we move our bodies, we increase our energy levels—an essential ingredient of an effective educator. We see the benefits of increased energy firsthand with students when we utilize active brain breaks as a way to increase attention and engagement, and this is also true for us as the adults. Every job position in our highly relationship-driven field demands a robust level of personal energy. Working in a school requires energy and often a lot of it. Energy begets energy, and so consciously incorporating movement into our daily lives is an essential need for us.

Movement includes *all* the ways we can move our bodies. For movement routines, consider what, when, and how you move your body. This might include how many steps you take throughout the day or how long you are on your feet as you avoid long periods of sitting.

Many of us spend more than nine hours sitting each day.[17] Following wise and healthy food choices and exercising thirty minutes a day are not enough to offset too many hours of sitting. So, make inactivity your enemy! Reducing the amount of time that we spend sitting down is more essential than brief but vigorous exercise.[18]

Physical movement includes both planned workouts as well as all the naturally occurring movement you engage in during your day. Remember, some is absolutely better than none, so don't get discouraged. Maybe you like to play on a sports league, attend exercise class twice a week (in person or online), or rack up miles on your stationary bike or out on the hiking trail—all of which are fantastic.

If you feel like you can't find time in your calendar for formalized workout sessions, remember that your daily steps and natural movements (bending, stretching, lunging, and standing) all count toward your overall physical wellness. Work to weave movement into your normal daily experiences as much as possible. The National Institute on Aging indicates that flexibility and balance are part of your physical health alongside activities of strength and endurance.[19]

As you are able, take more daily steps by parking farther away from the entrance to the grocery store, restaurant, school, or office. Embrace the stairs and avoid the escalators. Walk to talk with a colleague rather than send an email, or pace while you're on the phone. Before you know it, those steps on your smartwatch, Fitbit, or pedometer will start to climb!

Paying attention to movement helps us feel energized because by becoming aware of how and when we're moving, we're likely to add more movement to our day. We should participate in physical movement brain breaks alongside our students and strive to build movement breaks into our planning and team times as well. If a specific activity or workout is important to you, take the time to enjoy that activity as part of your life without feeling guilty or selfish. Put these activities on your daily calendar like any other appointment so you won't miss them because you're too hurried with other obligations.

Remember, being *busy* is a good thing. It means you are living a full life, which includes time for your movement routines. Being *hurried* is not so good. It means your food and movement routines drift into shallow and poor decision-making (a wellness routine in the next chapter) choices for your physical wellness, and before you know it, your sleep routines suffer as well. We dive deeper into the idea of a busy versus hurried life in chapter 2 (page 24).

As a team, allow movement routines to be part of your collaborative time together. Support one another's personal choices and goals for movement and build them into your team meeting agendas. Perhaps set some movement goals together. Consider a "70,000 steps a week challenge" for each team member. Log your steps each week and celebrate your successes. It doesn't have to be a competition, but rather a team wellness goal! One step, one day at a time.

MYWELLNESS ACTION

Sleep Routines

Sleep is the third routine for your physical wellness dimension. The way you feel when you are at school depends in large part on what happens when you are sleeping. Assistant director of health promotion and
wellness at Penn State Erin Raupers says, "If you are sleep-deprived, your memory will not be as good and you will not be able to learn efficiently or focus your attention."[21] Most people understand this. When we're not getting enough sleep, nothing seems to work right. According to the National Heart, Lung, and Blood Institute, when we sleep, our body is hard at work supporting healthy brain function and maintaining our physical health; this affects how well we "think, react, work, learn, and get along with others."[22] More than just affecting memory, sleep deficits impact our ability to remember information and how

Keep track of how much time you spend sitting in one day at work and at home. Are you above or below the national average of 9.3 hours per day?[20]

_____

_____

_____

_____

_____

_____

_____

_____

_____

_____

Name two actions you will take at work to improve your movement routines.

_____

_____

_____

_____

_____

_____

_____

_____

_____

_____

_____

_____

_____

_____

we interpret information. According to Gupta, a "well-rested brain is a healthy brain."[23]

Consider how prioritizing sleep acts as the cornerstone physical wellness routine for your food and movement routines. When you get enough sleep, you are much more likely to make food and movement choices that support your overall health and well-being.[24] Think about how much sleep you get each day and how you feel as a result. Are you perpetually exhausted or do you have the necessary energy you need to perform your job? Consider your sleep routines as you look for patterns and make connections to your mood and decision-making abilities in accordance with the amount and quality of your sleep.

On average, says human health and well-being expert Tom Rath, "the best performers sleep 8 hours and 36 minutes a day."[25] By comparison, the average American gets six hours and fifty-one minutes on weeknights, and over 30 percent of workers sleep fewer than six hours. Rath reminds us that "when you need an extra hour of energy, add an hour of sleep."[26]

In Japan, the phenomenon of *karoshi* means death brought on by extreme sleep deprivation; it has changed the way many Japanese companies are doing business.[27] While once known for its culture of long working hours, some Japanese workplaces are starting to reward workers who get a minimum of six hours of sleep per night and are adding napping rooms.[28]

It's important to note that this routine is about more than just nighttime sleeping hours. It also includes daytime rest. *Rest* means taking a small break during the workday—an essential component to avoid being hurried. As educators, our initial response to this might be, "I hardly have time to use the restroom. How can I possibly add rest to my day?"

Rest doesn't necessarily mean taking a nap. Rest during the day can include any stress-reducing activity like going for a quick walk around the building or the track (a benefit to your movement routine as well), doing a mindfulness meditation (more on this idea in chapter 3, page 44), or simply pausing for some deep breaths while looking away from the computer screen for a few minutes. You are taking a brief rest from the intensity of your workday. Working on a task too long can actually decrease your performance.[29] Instead, work your brain in bursts and take breaks as needed. This type of rest is essential for attention and for helping you feel more refreshed and restored—and it increases your creativity, which can inspire you as you work (often with colleagues) to create daily lessons and monthly unit plans, including a variety of student assessment and intervention materials and activities.[30]

Establishing both sleep *and* rest routines without guilt is essential to our educator wellness. As a team, share your best tips, tricks, and strategies for getting a good night's sleep, particularly as you navigate through different seasons of your life. For example, if you have young children at home, your sleep will most likely look very different than empty nesters'. Perhaps a veteran member of the team with grown children can share wisdom with teammates who have small children at home and are struggling to get adequate sleep. Or you could do a brief breathing exercise as a way to pause and rest throughout a long meeting or collaborative team session, as that is beneficial for everyone.

MY WELLNESS ACTION

Physical Wellness: Our Stories

Each dimension of wellness for educators tells a story about the ebb and flow for living our best lives. In this section of the chapter, we (Tina and Tim) briefly share some of our wellness stories and then invite you to write and share your wellness journey, too.

Tina's Story

Physical wellness is where I've made the most dramatic changes on my continual quest for overall health and well-being and is the wellness dimension I always recommend starting with. I know that when I prioritize and set boundaries around these three essential routines, I *feel* better. And when I feel better? I *am* better. I'm a better educator, partner, colleague, and friend. I'm far from perfect, but I've come a long way from where I once was in each of these routines. The positive impact of these changes on my life has been nothing short of incredible.

For me, this is the practice where feel-good self-care and educator wellness can sometimes collide. We've all been guilty of making choices in the name of self-care

Keep track of how much time you spend sleeping in one week. Are you above or below the average of six hours and fifty-one minutes per night?

_____

_____

_____

_____

_____

_____

_____

_____

_____

_____

Name two actions you will take at work to improve your nightly sleep routine.

_____

_____

_____

_____

_____

_____

_____

_____

_____

_____

_____

_____

_____

that don't actually serve our educator wellness. For example, staying up too late during the week to watch another TV episode might be a way we treat ourselves, and we call it *self-care*. This is a totally fine choice (in fact, it's absolutely *recommended*) every once in a while. However, when we do this every night, sacrificing precious sleep time, we're not treating ourselves at all; we're actually hurting ourselves. You walk around like a zombie because you're not sleeping enough, and this impacts your mood, decision making, and interactions with your students and colleagues.

It can be a tricky balance to find your own sweet spot here. It certainly takes practice to make choices that may not feel great in the moment but will help us feel fantastic in the long run—but we can absolutely do it. (If I can do it, I promise you can, too.) I've found that allowing myself to indulge more on the weekend while I stick to my wellness goals during the week is my personal sweet spot.

Another observation I have made is the awareness that my physical wellness depends on my daily habits. Establishing healthy habits around my food, movement, and sleep routines allows me to minimize the number of decisions I need to make each day, thus avoiding the dreaded decision fatigue state of mind discussed in chapter 2 (page 24). Of course, there is a time and a place for treats and indulgences that don't fall under my desired physical wellness goals, but those treats are the exception rather than the rule, which is what makes them *treats*.

Tim's Story

For the most part, I have spent my entire life living on the fringes of these three routines. Close to the extremes. Almost like a game to me. How much sleep do I need before my energy collapses? How often can I stray from the nutrient-rich foods and drinks fueling my body? How far can I push my various forms of movement before I collapse?

This fringe binging has caused me to live the same up-and-down physical wellness patterns over and over. I would drift toward less sleep, poorer food choices, or increased-intensity exercise routines to counterbalance the other two. And then I would see a picture of myself (or take a selfie) or catch myself at a drive-through for dinner on my way to another meeting, or worse yet, skip a workout.

I would seriously stop myself and have this conversation: "Well, Tim, you have to improve these routines or you will be no good to anyone. Your family needs you; your work needs you. You need to regain your energy and inspiration. Let's go! Start again on the first of the month." So, March first (or whatever month it was) would roll around, and once again, I would sleep seven hours a night, shun the drive-through food, have no late-night snacks, and stick to my workout routine. And as you can imagine, my new routines—the new me—lasted anywhere from one week to a few months, but never a full school season.

The daily grind of our profession would often wear me down. It was hard to get into a fixed routine during the school year when it felt as if my lesson design and delivery; formative and common assessment design and scoring; and the time and energy required by my interventions and constant communication with parents, students, and colleagues consumed every waking minute during the week (often bleeding into my weekend time with my family). The time I needed for positive food, movement, and sleep routines often felt selfish to me, and I would sacrifice my own well-being for the sake of others. Simply stated: I often placed my own physical health on the back burner.

Sometimes, however, you wake up to the reality of the choices you make. Our physical wellness routines are really internal choices. In my case, and as I document in my book *HEART!*, I had a heart attack at too young an age *because* I lived on the extremes of my food, movement, and sleep routines.[31] Yet, in some ways, my heart problems were a blessing. I don't have the choice to ignore my physical wellness routines anymore. My life depends on it.

To go deeper into this thinking and watch us (Tina and Tim) in conversation about this dimension of educator wellness, scan the QR code using your smartphone or device, or visit **go.SolutionTree.com/educatorwellness** to access the URLs for all videos.

Physical Wellness
www.SolutionTree.com/PhysicalWellness

Summarizing Thoughts

Working on our physical wellness isn't easy, and yet it is the foundation that pulls together our other dimensions of educator wellness. We are a highly relationship-driven, high-energy profession and therefore need to bring our best physical selves to work each day.

Remember these core takeaways regarding your daily physical wellness routines.

1. When we feel better, we are better.

2. Food, movement, and sleep are interconnected routines.

3. Choose food quality over quantity.

4. To sit or to stand? To move or not? Choose wisely.

5. Sleep, rest, repeat.

We invite you to consider this advice: when progress on your food, movement, and sleep routines seems slow, remember the wisdom James Clear offers in *Atomic Habits*: push yourself to consider how you can improve your physical wellness routines by just 1 percent tomorrow.[32] Think incremental improvements: one action, one small step today, for a bigger goal tomorrow. If you find yourself doubting your progress, invite a trusted friend to join you on the journey. Find joy in the small victories along the way.

Now it is your turn!

Physical Wellness: Your Story

Now that you have read this chapter, answered the My Wellness Action prompts, and considered parts of our (Tim and Tina's) stories, what does physical wellness mean to you?

Take some time to write about your personal physical wellness story. Don't worry if you don't consider yourself a writer. This isn't about the writing; it's about the reflection. You can use the prompts we provide or you can simply write your own story and your next steps for moving your physical wellness forward in your professional life. Consider placing a date and time by each entry as you tell your wellness story, and reference figure B.1 (page 84) as needed.

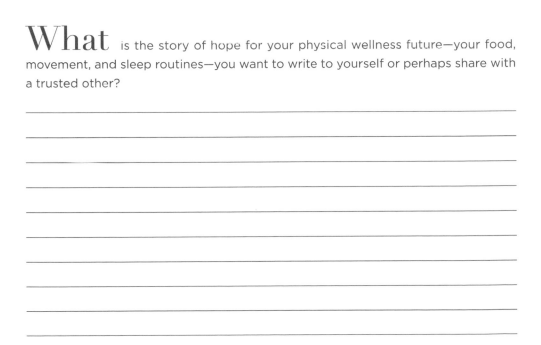

What is the story of hope for your physical wellness future—your food, movement, and sleep routines—you want to write to yourself or perhaps share with a trusted other?

_____

_____

_____

_____

_____

_____

_____

_____

_____

_____

_____

_____

_____

_____

_____

_____

_____

_____

_____

_____

Examine the list of summarizing thoughts (pages 19–20). Of the five ideas listed, which one do you need to focus on in the next few months? Write out two *I will* statements to help with your growth in the physical dimension of your life.

_____

_____

_____

_____

_____

_____

_____

_____

_____

_____

_____

_____

_____

_____

_____

_____

_____

_____

Consider current progress in your physical wellness dimension. How do you anticipate your progress in your food, movement, and sleep routines will impact your relationships with students and colleagues during the school year?

_____

_____

_____

_____

_____

_____

_____

_____

_____

_____

_____

_____

_____

_____

_____

_____

_____

_____

Be patient and know small tweaks and minor changes can add up quickly. You don't have to change it all in one day; in fact, you can't change it all in one day. You simply need to get started. There will be setbacks, and that's OK. Give yourself a wellness plan that allows a gradual buildup for sustaining a new routine most days. And as you do that, there will be a positive impact on the stressors in your work life. The mental wellness dimension of our work life is next!

CHAPTER 2

The Mental Wellness Dimension

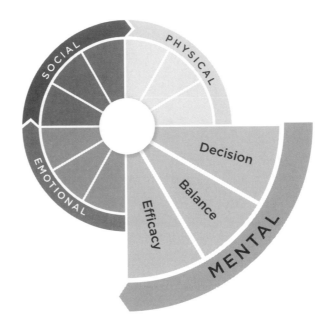

To be steady while the world spins around you. To act without frenzy. To hear only what needs to be heard. To process quietude—exterior and interior— on command.

—Ryan Holiday

Adversity, *stress, exhaustion, fatigue, weariness,* and *burnout.* Tough words.

These obstacles lurk around every corner during the school year. The world can spin around us pretty fast sometimes. The margin between being busy and fully engaged in daily life, compared to being hurried and unengaged in life, is razor thin.

According to the World Health Organization (WHO), your mental wellness is a "state of well-being in which the individual realizes his or her own abilities, can cope with the normal stresses of life, can work productively and fruitfully, and is able to make a contribution to his or her community."[33] Translating WHO's words to your everyday school life, your mental wellness as an educator might read something like this: "A state of well-being in which we successfully cope with the stressors of life and realize our work-life self-efficacy—our belief and confidence in our capabilities to help every student learn."

And you are expected to do this day after day. On your best days and on days when adversity at home or at work swings into your pathway. Thankfully, there are preemptive and self-regulatory routines you can embrace to help you cope with the stress, high energy, unexpected adversity, and relentless demands of your work life. You can avoid the prolonged stress and frustration that can lead to mental exhaustion. Adversity need not steal your joy or burn you out.

In short, stress is OK. *Prolonged* stress, not so much.

Some stress can actually help the immune system and protect your body from infection.[34] Successfully coping with your stress leaves you tired at the end of each day, but fired up for another round tomorrow. The number of activities on your professional plate and your capability to handle them well is a good feeling and exists as part of your internal professional life balance. You are not bored for sure, and on most days, you do not generally experience high levels of anxiety.

Too much stress, however, can be problematic. Stress that persists for weeks or months can weaken the immune system and cause issues like fatigue, anxiety, depression, high blood pressure, and even heart disease.[35] Words like *burnout* or *exhaustion* can creep into our thoughts.

Write about current actions that best help you to avoid drifting away from a positive sense of mental well-being each day.

_____

_____

_____

_____

_____

_____

_____

_____

_____

_____

_____

_____

_____

_____

_____

_____

_____

_____

_____

_____

_____

_____

_____

_____

_____

Burnout, as referenced by the WHO, is:

A syndrome conceptualized as resulting from chronic workplace stress that has not been successfully managed. It is characterized by three dimensions:

- feelings of energy depletion or exhaustion;
- increased mental distance from one's job, or feelings of negativism or cynicism related to one's job; and
- reduced professional efficacy.

Burn-out refers specifically to phenomena in the occupational context and should not be applied to describe experiences in other areas of life.[36]

There are key words and phrases in WHO's definition, including _chronic stress, energy depletion, mentally distancing from the work_, and _sense of reduced efficacy_. These words and phrases are indicators you are on the road to prolonged stress. Are you working longer hours each day or every weekend? Are you struggling to catch up on all the work-related tasks that need to get done? Are you easily irritated by others, and often cynical or negative in your communication? Do you gradually lose time in the week for your family, for fun downtime activities, and for personal quiet reflection time, or worse, sacrifice your own time for your physical wellness sleep and movement routines (chapter 1, page 8)? You can feel a sense of dispassion for the work looming ahead.

Yet, you can avoid the drift toward prolonged mental stress and exhaustion. When you feel mentally well, you work more productively with and for your students and colleagues, enjoy free time more, contribute more actively in your community, and are more likely to practice routines of self-care and kindness.[37]

MY WELLNESS ACTION

The mental wellness dimension of the Wellness Solutions for Educators framework (page 81) brings into focus three routines for improvement that can help you avoid the drift away from a positive sense of your mental well-being each day: (1) decision, (2) balance, and (3) efficacy routines. These routines can help you bring the best and most confident version of yourself, your knowledge, and your positive energy to your students and colleagues each day.

Decision Routines

Take a quick guess: how many decisions do you think you make each day?

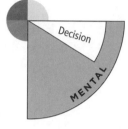

Got it? Hold on to that answer for a bit. We'll give you a number in a moment.

To answer this question, consider the nature of your daily decisions and choices *before* work—everything from what you will wear, what you need to do for your family, what you will eat for breakfast and lunch, whether you should get gas for your car on the way to work, which route you should take, and where you left your keys.

How about your decisions and choices *at* school? Which students need more of your time; which families do you need to call or email; what do you need to take to your team meeting today; when will you grade those student papers; what do you need for your mentoring meeting tomorrow; how should you change this lesson since the students seem lost; do you join that meeting after school today, grade those papers, or do both at the same time?

These types of decisions represent the planned part of your day; there are also in-the-moment decisions related to incidents such as an unexpected student behavior problem, a suddenly angry colleague who needs to talk *now*, or a text with an urgent request for help.

Our professional responsibilities call on us to make many difficult (and wise) decisions. The sheer volume of those decisions can be exhausting and comes with a name: *decision fatigue*.

Social psychologist Roy F. Baumeister describes decision fatigue as the "emotional and mental strain resulting from a burden of choices."[38] As educators, we face more than 1,500 decisions per day at work and over 35,000 for the entire day![39] Surprised? We were! Was that number close to your guess? Worse yet, as the day wears on, our decision-making wisdom wears down, sapping our physical and mental energy due to the sheer volume of our choices and decisions.

Thus, as a default position, the brain starts taking shortcuts, and either we make decisions impulsively (not wise), such as sending a late-night email we regret the next day, or we avoid decision making altogether as we mindlessly scroll through our phones on various social media apps.[40]

Yet, our need to make good decisions is an essential aspect of our job. So, what can we do? How can we avoid decision fatigue?

First, consider your daily habits. Create daily habits and rituals that provide some comfort and reduce the number of decisions you have to make each day. Because so much of our job requires us to make in-the-moment decisions, it's essential to regulate and automate anything that we can regulate and automate.

For example, consider going to bed at the same time each night and waking at the same time each morning. Create a ritual around preparing for the next day by taking a moment to get your work bag ready, lay out your clothes, pack your lunch and gym bags, and put your car keys next to your work keys. At school, consider parking in the same location, responding to emails and returning calls at a certain time, or grading student papers and designing lesson plans at the same time each day. Incorporate some of the mindfulness practices from chapter 3 (page 44) to help adjust to unexpected events and situations that will undoubtedly come up.

If you are a teacher newer to the profession, rely on your more expert and time-savvy colleagues, such as your mentor teacher, to help with ideas for more efficient daily working routines. For in-depth guidance and a reproducible template, "Action Plan to Organize Daily Tasks," to support improved decision-making habits, you can refer to the book *Coaching for Educator Wellness: A Guide to Supporting New and Experienced Teachers.*[41]

Second, establish firm boundaries around your time at work. Do not let others hijack control of your time through activities you were not asked to do in advance. Work with your team and colleagues to reasonably reduce the number of decisions you must make each week regarding timelines and due dates for materials, meeting locations, and meeting agendas, and expectations for shared duties with your colleagues. Do not allow a forty-five-minute team meeting to drift into a seventy-five-minute session. Start and end on time. Honor your team meeting norms.

Third, be sure to take time that's just for you. Schedule self-care into your calendar just like you would a meeting or an appointment. Self-care can include everything from daily stress-reducing activities such as the physical movement routines from chapter 1 (page 8), morning coffee with your quiet thoughts, a yoga class in the afternoon, stretch breaks throughout the day, or a walk around the outside of the school before you head home. Do not allow yourself to miss self-care moments in the name of crossing something else off your to-do list.

The practice of self-compassion is an interesting aspect of our decision making. *Self-compassion* facilitates a healthy decision-making response to coping with adversity by moderating our reaction to negative events. Kristin Neff, of the Department of Educational Psychology at the University of Texas at Austin, and her colleague Christopher Germer, from Harvard, provide insight: "Self-compassion, therefore, involves being touched by and open to one's own suffering, not avoiding or disconnecting from it, and generating the desire to alleviate one's own suffering and to heal oneself with kindness."[42]

Neff and Germer also say:

> Individuals higher in [the] trait self-compassion demonstrated less extreme reactions, less negative emotions, more accepting thoughts, and a greater tendency to put their problems into perspective, while at the same time acknowledging their own responsibility.[43]

Self-compassion, then, is another daily decision we make. A decision to acknowledge our responsibility for avoiding the drift from a busy to a hurried life. To realize that no matter how good we may be at making those 35,000 decisions every day, their sheer volume can overwhelm us sometimes. To give our inner voice permission to say, "Today I gave it my best, and it is good enough, for *now*. Tomorrow, however, I'll strive to be just a bit better." In those moments, give yourself some self-compassion, some kindness, and less self-judgment and get ready to live your best life tomorrow.

Think about your decision-making routines and the concepts of automation, regulation, boundaries, and self-compassion. How do *you* avoid becoming exhausted from all the decisions you must make each day?

MY WELLNESS ACTION

Identify two or three new routines for automating or regulating more of your daily decisions.

_____
_____
_____
_____
_____
_____
_____
_____
_____
_____
_____
_____
_____
_____
_____
_____
_____
_____
_____
_____
_____
_____
_____
_____
_____
_____
_____

Which of the busy-versus-hurried-life descriptors best indicate your current state of well-being *today*? Are you busy, hurried, or somewhere in between the two? Describe how you try to avoid the hurried life.

_____

_____

_____

_____

_____

_____

_____

_____

_____

_____

_____

_____

_____

_____

_____

_____

_____

_____

_____

_____

_____

_____

Balance Routines

Consider your day-to-day activities. Are you busy? Or are you hurried?

To some extent, our profession is designed for us to live full and busy lives. Every day is packed with students and colleagues and the relational energy they bring to the workplace. We find our purpose and meaning in the daily good we do for others and all of the wonderful and sometimes painful stories, attitudes, beliefs, feelings, and daily moods of every student and colleague in our path. Every day brings some surprise and nuance that needs our attention and love. We are busy in our workplace for sure. Yet we need to be aware of that thin margin between a busy life and an out-of-control hurried life.

Busy is good; hurried is not so good. Consider these comparisons.

- Busy: I have a full schedule of daily activities.
- Hurried: I am unable to be fully present due to too many competing demands.

- Busy: I dedicate daily time for quiet reflection.
- Hurried: There are too many demands on my time for daily reflection.

- Busy: My job is demanding; I love it!
- Hurried: I feel physically and emotionally drained every day. My job is dragging me down.

- Busy: I cannot do my job without the help of others.
- Hurried: I just don't have time to work with others. Isolation is easier.

●MYWELLNESS ACTION

How did you respond to the My Wellness Action prompt? Was it a good, full, busy day or a not-so-good, hurried day? We have many tasks and expectations placed on the many plates we are spinning, and for the most part, we have the skill and the will to balance them well.

Then one day, we notice ourselves a bit more on a ragged edge. Colleagues ask us why we seem so short tempered, angry, defensive, and anxious lately. The speed of expectations forces us into a faster mode of life. Time is fixed and there is not enough of it anymore. Our energy, usually endless, seems depleted. We feel as if we are unbalanced, and the demands of our work and home life are cutting into our daily energy and engagement with others. Often, people we trust might notice our hurried-life drift before we do. Be sure to use their words of wisdom and input as needed to help you maintain high positive energy. You can renew your daily energy by being more intentional with a few balance routines built into your daily life.

First, hang out with exceptionally inspiring people. This might sound simple, yet it is important. On days you sense you might be drifting into the hurried life, is there someone you can count on to bring you back into a high-energy, positive state of well-being? Is there some-one in your life who generally inspires you and—directly or indirectly, by their actions—inspires you toward more balanced life pursuits? Perhaps there is also a colleague, friend, or family member willing to be a go-to person when you sense you are drifting into the hurried life. Perhaps your relationship is mutually nourishing and you can do the same for that person as well.

Second, consider events at work that are exceptionally inspiring to you. Is there an event involving your students or colleagues that has you walking away inspired, with a renewed sense of energy for your work life? When you find your energy being depleted by your workload, take a break and be intentional about attending those inspirational events. Consider events highlighting student effort and energy, remind-ing you why you are doing the work you do.

Third, pay attention to your physical wellness routines from chapter 1 (page 8). Give yourself a break from the intensity of your day with movement: a thirty-minute walk or time for the quiet zone of that yoga class or any other form of exercise that appeals to you. There is a renewable mental and physical energy benefit to the rest of your day.

Fourth, pay attention to your working environment. How your class-room or office space looks and feels can lift your energy levels for the day. Make it a place with photos and artifacts that make you feel calm, confident, and valued. Consider such things as extra lighting, colors, music, exhibits honoring your heritage, and more. Do you like a clut-tered classroom or office space, or do you prefer neat and orderly?

How does your work environment lift you up and into an increased high-energy and positive mental state each day?

Fifth, have an inspiring recreation or hobby outside of your work world. Maybe you play drums for a country-western band, write poetry, weave baskets, bird-watch, sing in the local choir, play softball, or work in a summer circus. Whatever the activity, just make it something outside of our profession, and with friends (from in our profession or not) who love you just for you and not what you do for a living. Those friends will supply unconditional love, provide balance against the stress of your work life, and help you renew your energy supply for work.

This list of renewable energy ideas is helpful, yet the list provides *external* actions and routines we can use to avoid the thin line between being busy and being hurried. More important, however, we can obtain an improved high-energy state when we allow our brains to rest and recover from all of the *noise* of each day. We seek *internal* balance. We need time for complete silence and solitude from the noise *each day*.

Sherry Turkle is a Massachusetts Institute of Technology professor and founding director of the MIT Initiative on Technology and Self. Turkle indicates:

> How do you get from connection to isolation? You end up isolated if you don't cultivate the capacity for solitude, the ability to be separate, to gather yourself. Solitude is where you find yourself so that you can reach out to other people and form real attachments. When we don't have the capacity for solitude, we turn to other people in order to feel less anxious or in order to feel alive. When this happens, we're not able to appreciate who they are. It's as though we're using them as spare parts to support our fragile sense of self.[44]

In her studies, Turkle verifies that the door to successful relationships is *purposeful* solitude, with an embraced silence (especially regarding our technologies).

Author Ryan Holiday verifies solitude as necessary to reduce the daily noise from our lives and bring greater clarity to our work-life balance:

> It is difficult to think clearly in rooms filled with other people. It's difficult to understand yourself if you are never by yourself . . . Sometime[s] you have to disconnect in order to better connect with yourself and with the people you serve and love.[45]

Stillness built into your daily life provides the necessary balance between high-positive-energy and some low-positive-energy time each day. It is with this balance that you avoid the drift into a high-negative state of energy (the hurried life) at work. Seek a time for reflection and quiet. Stillness is the gateway to increased high-positive and unhurried energy. Do not try to escape the silence. Embrace it. See it as a gift for a better you tomorrow.

Use your quiet time to manage the ebb and flow of your life and to reflect on how to stay busy but balanced. Move away from the stress of the day, disengage from your professional life, and benefit from some quiet processing time that can provide clarity to the question, Are you busy or hurried? Choose a time and place every day to practice fifteen total minutes of quietude. Quiet and silence. No noise, no music, no phone. Sit, stand, walk, or write. Give your brain the gift of silence. To do so, you can use some of the mindfulness activities described in chapter 3 (page 44).

MY WELLNESS ACTION

Efficacy Routines

What do you think of when you hear or see the word *efficacy*? Our (Tim and Tina's) sense of efficacy as collaborators is rooted in our *evidence of success* through our work together. Stanford professor  emeritus and psychologist Albert Bandura helps us understand the idea of efficacy as it applies to our work life. Bandura's concept of self-efficacy derives from his social-cognitive theory of behavioral change.[46] Self-efficacy refers to your *accurate* belief in your capabilities (your competence and confidence) to successfully cope with tasks and obligations. In our profession, as teachers and leaders, we hope to successfully cope with the task and obligation of helping every student learn.

Self-efficacy, then, is developed through evidence of your competence and confidence. For example, you might observe your competence through successful student performance data on a specific standard. You

Name one busy-but-balanced routine that works best for you. Name one new action you can begin now to help you avoid the hurried life.

_____

_____

_____

_____

_____

_____

_____

_____

_____

_____

_____

_____

_____

_____

_____

_____

_____

_____

_____

_____

_____

_____

might observe student success during a carefully designed lesson—you thought the lesson would be great but weren't sure. Effectively using a new technology to promote formative student learning as part of your assessments might increase your confidence in using the technology. It is, in fact, competence that moves us closer to understanding just how much we do *not yet* know. And it is confidence in what we do know that moves us closer to taking positive action each day—not resting on our old knowledge.

Your self-efficacy (competence and confidence) evaluation is rooted in whether your students are successful, whether you exhibit high positive energy and perseverance at work each day, the degree to which your decision-making and balance routines are wise and sustained during times of adversity, and your willingness to embrace change and a growth mindset.

Thus, you are confident and competent enough to act on what you do know, yet humble enough to challenge and improve on your current knowledge base, recognizing there is still much you do not know. You learn to strike just the right balance "between arrogance (assuming we know more than we do) and insecurity (believing we know too little to act)."[47]

Self-efficacy, then, represents a decision-making line that separates us from the road to burnout and exhaustion. Award-winning psychologist Ethan Kross provides insight into how we can use our inner voice to help us with competence and confidence development in our daily routines. In his book *Chatter: The Voice in Our Head, Why It Matters, and How to Harness It*, Kross describes how we talk to ourselves and listen to what we say, and explains how to avoid a negative voice that can become what he calls *chatter*:

> Chatter consists of the cyclical negative thoughts and emotions that turn our singular capacity for introspection into a curse rather than a blessing. It puts our performance, decision making, relationships, happiness, and health in jeopardy. We think about that screwup at work or misunderstanding with a loved one and end up flooded by how bad we feel. Then we think about it again. And again.[48]

Is there a roadblock causing you to lose some of your own confidence and sense of competence at work as well? Is it possible your self-efficacy as a teacher and leader is spinning around a negative cycle of chatter in your head? Perhaps the majority of your students were not successful *again* on a specific quiz, test, or performance assignment. Perhaps there is opposition to your proposal for a more engaging student lesson design for your course, or your grade-level team is consistently in conflict and blaming others, despite your best efforts.

Or perhaps the inner voice is more subtle. Your students' performance results are decent, but not as good as those of other team members'. There are certain academic content strategies or teaching pedagogies you just don't know about, or don't seem to know as well as your colleagues, at least. Despite the evidence to the contrary (your students love you and they *are* reasonably successful), you feel as if you are failing. That inner voice whispers, *not good enough*. Your belief in your capabilities to impact student learning takes a hit. What can you do?

Thankfully, Kross provides several strategies (he describes them as *tools*) to combat the chatter that can tear away at the fabric of our sense of self-efficacy. Here are a few of Kross's strategies with our (Tim and Tina's) take on them.[49]

- **Imagine advising a friend:** When adversity strikes and the tasks you are expected to accomplish begin to challenge your confidence or competence, step away from the chatter in your head and ask, "What would I say to my colleague having the same doubts? How would I encourage a colleague in this same situation?" You are more likely to be much kinder to your friend and colleague than you are to yourself. When you feel as if your self-efficacy is taking a prolonged sideroad, give yourself the same kind advice and self-compassion you would give your colleague or friend.

- **Normalize your experiences:** You will fail at times, and every day won't be a great day. Yes, you will have your doubts. Who doesn't? Your colleagues have the exact same types of doubts you do. You are, for sure, not alone in the adversity boat! It helps to recognize you are part of the greater humanity of all educators. (Have you noticed how often we—Tina and Tim—write using the word *we*? As in, when we make a mistake, we embrace the error. The word *we* allows us to realize that our times of doubt are not unique, because we are part of a greater humanity. We are indeed in a pretty big boat—together.)

- **Reframe your experiences as a challenge:** Reframing sounds easy in theory, but in reality, it is not! Remember when COVID-19 surfaced? In the beginning, the pandemic presented an almost impossible set of overwhelming circumstances. It presented a threat to the way we think and act as teachers and leaders—as educators. The key to sustaining your self-efficacy through any real or perceived

Give yourself permission to be grateful. End each day describing the best parts of your day. Write it down and say it out loud—to yourself or to others.

_____
_____
_____
_____
_____
_____
_____
_____
_____
_____
_____
_____
_____
_____
_____
_____
_____
_____
_____
_____
_____
_____
_____
_____
_____
_____
_____
_____

threat, such as the COVID-19 pandemic, is to reframe it, or view it as a challenge you can manage through your own confidence and competence development.

By the late 1990s, Bandura expanded on his self-efficacy work to establish that collective efficacy can impact and improve our individual self-efficacy.[50] Thus, our personal confidence and competence for meeting the many demands and expectations of our jobs improve because of the modeling we observe from our colleagues, as well as the sharing of our collective wisdom. How to become a great team member and benefit from the experiences of collective team efficacy is discussed in chapter 4 (page 62).

Finally, Bandura describes how your degree of self-efficacy can affect whether you think pessimistically or optimistically, how well you persevere and succeed in the face of difficulties, and how well you improve the quality of your daily decisions.[51] One way to think more optimistically and persevere in your work is to be aware of all the students and colleagues who are the beneficiaries of your self-efficacy efforts. You can do this by increasing your gratitude routines. Practicing gratitude reduces depression and anxiety, lowers stress, and increases happiness and empathy, acting like a big reset button and giving your brain a time-out.[52]

Consider the three mental wellness routines discussed for this dimension: (1) decision, (2) balance, and (3) efficacy. You can show gratitude for the decisions you need to make each day, knowing the impact you will have on so many students and colleagues. You can consider gratitude for balancing a high-positive-energy work life with low-positive-energy quiet time. And you can consider gratitude for knowing you can be *both* competent and confident while simultaneously recognizing there is still so much you do not know.

 M Y WELLNESS ACTION

Mental Wellness: Our Stories

Each dimension of wellness for educators tells a story about the ebb and flow for living our best lives. In this section of the chapter, we (Tina and Tim) briefly share some of our wellness stories and then invite you to write and share your wellness journey, too.

Tim's Story

My first thought about mental health and wellness is *MTXE*. I first encountered this acronym in high school, it stayed with me in college, and then it became a major part of my attempts to teach with inspiration over the years.

In some ways, MTXE helped me overcome what I often felt was a lack of talent and self-confidence. During my early years of teaching (about years one through ten), I was driven to reach success with my students, yet I often felt frazzled. Without my self-awareness, mental exhaustion and emotional exhaustion hung out in the doorway of my classroom.

And then one evening, late at work (after 6 p.m.), a close friend and teaching colleague I had great respect for sat down in my classroom and said, "I can't keep up. I am taking a few personal days. And I need a few days away from this grind."

She left my room and I sat there thinking about how she always had her act together. How could *she* be exhausted? I also realized I was too close to that same danger of prolonged exhaustion. I didn't want to be exhausted all of the time, either, and pretend as if everything were OK.

I took out a pad of paper and I wrote down a list of all of the responsibility plates I was spinning at the moment. I had headers on my list like husband, father, graduate school, professional work at school, professional work outside of school (textbook writing), church activities, coaching (my kids') sports activities, my own physical health, house and yard maintenance, and more. Under each heading, I wrote down all of the activities, pressures, and anxieties that came with doing each of them really well.

And I came to two conclusions. First, no wonder I felt mentally exhausted. I had been thinking I could balance these various spinning plates and corresponding activities. I could be a superhero to everyone, and in my inner voice, I embraced that feeling of being a hero.

The second revelation was much harsher. As I examined this long list of columns on my notepad, I had to face the reality that many of these spinning plates were crashing to the floor. I was, at best, giving shallow responses to my home life and my work life. I had drifted right through busy to the downside of hurried. All in the name of MTXE.

What is MTXE, you might wonder? It stands for *m*ental *t*oughness and e*x*tra *e*ffort. It is a great motto, and it helped me overcome many obstacles in my life along the way. And it does conjure up an image of owning my own destiny. My self-efficacy.

Looking back and moving forward, I have changed that motto to MTXE R&B. No, not rhythm and blues. I have shifted and improved on my MTXE engaging-life-to-the-fullest drive with the caveat of *r*eflection and *b*alance. I have been working on this a long time now. And the R&B part eludes me from time to time, but because I have embraced routines of decision making, balance, and self-efficacy through daily reflection (such as simply writing it all down on a notepad), I am keeping any chance for prolonged exhaustion where it belongs—far off in the distance.

Tina's Story

Like so many of us, when the COVID-19 pandemic rocked our world in March 2020, I felt incredible stress and my mental wellness took a serious hit. Nearly every workshop and speaking engagement on my calendar for the next few months was cancelled or postponed, and I had no idea what the future held. I was afraid of the virus, unsure of what would happen with my job, worried about my family and friends, and horrified by the idea of being quarantined forever. My stress caused me to have more than a few sleepless nights and I consumed (way) more carbs and sugar than I'd like to admit.

As the days turned into weeks and the weeks turned into months, my stress moved into the dreaded *prolonged* category. I knew I needed to take control of my mental wellness when I recognized my personal symptoms of distress and anxiety showing up on a daily basis: I was having trouble concentrating, I felt fatigued most of the day, I was irritable and struggling with mood swings, and my sleep (and sugar consumption) wasn't getting any better. I knew I couldn't continue like this forever, even as the pandemic seemed to stretch on with no end in sight.

I re-established my healthy physical wellness routines by making food choices that supported my health goals (I got all of the added sugar out of my house and started cooking more), committing to daily exercise (my husband and I started taking long walks together and purchased new road bikes), and prioritizing sleep first and foremost (less Netflix, more books before bed). I created a daily schedule and put my energy into things I could control: converting my on-site workshops to engaging virtual sessions, starting my next book, and tackling a long-held goal of starting my own podcast.

And it worked.

I started sleeping again, I felt rested and more energized, I was a kinder and gentler human, and I felt a greater sense of peace even though so much was uncertain. I learned so many lessons about myself during this time, particularly the importance of attending to mental wellness and how physical wellness acts as the foundation for this work.

To go deeper into this thinking and watch us (Tina and Tim) in conversation about this dimension of educator wellness, scan the QR code using your smartphone or device, or visit **go.SolutionTree.com/educatorwellness** to access the URLs for all videos.

Mental Wellness
www.SolutionTree.com/MentalWellness

Summarizing Thoughts

Working on our mental wellness and avoiding exhaustion is a daily push and pull, ebb and flow, throughout our working lifetime. Self-regulating our time will serve our positive high-energy needs so we can do our jobs well every day. We are a highly relation-driven, high-energy profession. As such, we need to bring our best mental selves to work each day.

Remember these core takeaways regarding your daily mental wellness routines.

1. Thirty-five-thousand decisions a day! Automate and regulate!

2. Respect the line between busy and hurried.

3. Balance positive high-energy actions with positive low-energy quiet time.

4. Be competent and confident while improving.

5. Practice daily gratitude, especially on your worst days.

We invite you to consider this advice: when your self-confidence is low and you find yourself doubting your competence, reframe it as a challenge and see it as an opportunity for growth.[53] And finally, embrace your imperfections as part of your humanity. Find joy in the lifelong journey of a busy, full, reflective, and risk-taking life of learning.

Now it is your turn!

Mental Wellness: Your Story

Your professional life thrives when you reflect on and work to gradually improve your routines for mental wellness. You can measure your wellness progress based on the three distinct routines—(1) decision, (2) balance, and (3) efficacy—for embracing the rewards of good stress and avoiding the exhaustion of prolonged stress. Now that you have read this chapter, answered the My Wellness Action prompts, and considered parts of our (Tim and Tina's) educator wellness stories, what does the mental wellness dimension mean to you, based on your experiences?

Take some time to write about your personal mental wellness story. Don't worry if you don't consider yourself a writer. This isn't about the writing; it's about the reflection. You can use the prompts we provide or simply write your own story and next steps for improving the mental wellness dimension in your professional life. Consider placing a date and time by each entry as you tell your wellness story, and reference figure B.2 (page 85) as needed.

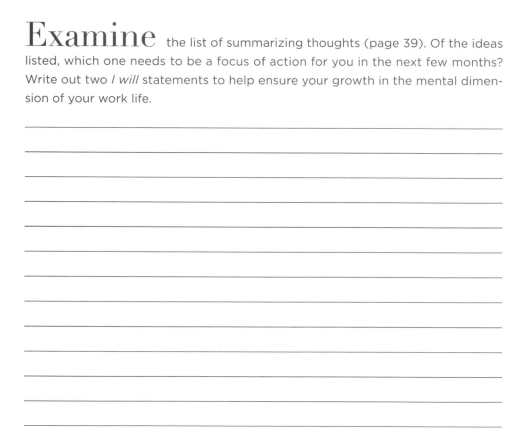

Examine the list of summarizing thoughts (page 39). Of the ideas listed, which one needs to be a focus of action for you in the next few months? Write out two *I will* statements to help ensure your growth in the mental dimension of your work life.

_____

_____

_____

_____

_____

Consider current progress in your mental wellness dimension. Identify symptoms that let you know your daily life is no longer balanced. You can feel yourself moving from a busy to a hurried life. Name two or three specific routines you are using to automate and regulate your decisions as well.

_____

_____

_____

_____

_____

_____

_____

_____

_____

_____

_____

_____

_____

_____

_____

_____

_____

_____

_____

_____

How are you doing with your physical wellness routines progress from chapter 1 (page 8)? What, if any, connections can you make between your physical and mental wellness routines?

_____

_____

_____

_____

_____

_____

_____

_____

_____

_____

_____

_____

_____

_____

_____

_____

_____

_____

_____

_____

_____

_____

_____

What is the story of hope for your mental wellness future—your decision, balance, and efficacy routines—you want to write to yourself or perhaps share with a trusted other?

_____

_____

_____

_____

_____

_____

_____

_____

_____

_____

_____

_____

_____

_____

_____

_____

_____

_____

_____

_____

_____

_____

_____

_____

_____

_____

_____

_____

_____

_____

_____

As educators, our physical and mental wellness stories unfold as we walk through each day. We can be the authors of those stories. Be patient and know minor changes in your decision-making routines and balance activities not only add up quickly, they will impact your emotional wellness, too. And that educator wellness dimension is next!

CHAPTER 3

The Emotional Wellness Dimension

All learning has an emotional base.

—Plato

Our emotions matter.

Our emotions are ever present; they are with us all the time. Our emotions are our states of feeling.[54] Pause for a moment to get in tune with your current emotions. Use the margin space and jot down your emotions in this moment. For example, are you sad, tired, angry, happy, tender, calm, or something else?

Our emotional wellness matters just as much as our physical and mental wellness. Not only do our emotions impact our overall mood and how our day goes, our emotions are associated with less stress and burnout and also greater job satisfaction.[55] The term *emotional intelligence* was first described by researchers Peter Salovey and John Mayer in 1990.[56] Psychologist Daniel Goleman subsequently extended and popularized the meaning of emotional intelligence in the mid-1990s.[57]

According to the Institute for Health and Human Potential, our emotional intelligence is the ability to "recognize, understand and manage our own emotions" and also "recognize, understand and influence the emotions of others."[58]

In addition, research out of the Yale Center for Emotional Intelligence shows that when a teacher possesses emotional wellness, students cause fewer disruptions, are more focused, and perform better academically.[59] When we are able to recognize, understand, and manage our emotions, we increase our overall impact on students and colleagues. Whether we're interacting with students, colleagues, or families, it's important to consider our emotions and the nature of our responses to them.

Building our emotional wellness includes being aware of how we feel each day; understanding why we feel that way; and reflecting on how we teach, interact with, and lead others, including how we self-regulate our responses to others. Consider a time when a student erupted and disrupted your work life. A *reaction* might be to begin yelling at the student in front of the class, while a *response* might be to guide the student to a safe place where you can help to de-escalate the student's actions. Or perhaps a parent loses her patience during a meeting. A *reaction* might be to get angry and raise your voice in an attempt to establish power, while a *response* might be to take a few deep breaths while you listen before speaking.

In *Managing the Inner World of Teaching*, education researchers Robert J. Marzano and Jana S. Marzano point out:

> While it will always be important to keep abreast of teaching behaviors and instructional strategies that have the greatest

chance of enhancing students' learning, there is another
aspect of effective teaching that has been virtually ignored
in the literature on classroom instruction: the relationship
between what teachers are thinking and feeling at any
point in time and their actions at that same point in time.[60]

Our emotions are tied to our actions and reactions, both inside and outside the classroom, and are essential to student learning. Why is a routine of understanding our emotions and then using thoughtful reflection and regulation so important? Because our positive response to our emotions becomes a portal to cognition and learning for students.

Consider this insight from educators and researchers Carol Ann Tomlinson and David A. Sousa when assessing the work of brain researchers Chai M. Tyng, Hafeez U. Amin, Mohamad N. M. Saad, and Aamir S. Malik:

Much recent research in neuroscience has focused on the
influence emotion has on learning. Structures in the limbic
system generate emotions, which are then moderated
by the frontal lobe's control functions. Emotions have a
strong influence on attention—and attention drives what
the student's brain decides to learn or ignore. Emotions
also modulate long-term memory, and thus can enhance or
impair what is stored there. When new learning has minimal
or no emotional component, the chances of long-term
memory consolidation and storage are low.[61]

As Tomlinson and Sousa point out, while our negative response to our emotions can shut down our students' cognition and learning, our positive response to our emotions reinforces or strengthens memory, enhances learning as a social interaction, and develops empathy for others. Thus, developmental foundations of cultural learning in the brain's prefrontal and motor regions may serve as "neural precursors to compassionate feeling and actions during adolescence."[62] The way we model our emotions and our responses to them affects our students' and colleagues' attention and learning.

As educators, we work to develop emotional intelligence in our students, but sometimes neglect to improve our own emotional intelligence. Indeed, the Collaborative for Academic, Social, and Emotional

Learning defines social-emotional learning this way:

> The process through which all young people *and adults* acquire and apply the knowledge, skills and attitudes to develop healthy identities, manage emotions and achieve personal and collective goals, feel and show empathy for others, establish and maintain supportive relationships, and make responsible and caring decisions.[63]

The italics are ours, to emphasize the importance of including adults in our social-emotional work in schools.

Improving our emotional wellness is a forever pursuit. We will have good days, better days, and some not-so-good emotional days. At its core, emotional wellness is the third dimension of the Wellness Solutions for Educators framework (page 81) and involves three routines—(1) awareness, (2) understanding, and (3) mindfulness—that build on one another. First, we build awareness around our daily emotions, and then we work to build understanding around why we experience certain emotions in specific situations. Finally, we develop mindfulness routines that help us respond to and cope with the wide nature of our full range of emotions as we advance toward the goal of living our best lives as educators.

Awareness Routines

At the beginning of this chapter, we asked you to consider your emotions at the moment you were reading the opening. Revisit what you recorded; say your emotions out loud. Hear them. Become aware of them. According to Marc Brackett, the director of the Yale Center for Emotional Intelligence:

> Our emotions are an important source of information about what's going on inside us. Our multiple senses bring us news from our bodies, our minds, and the outside world, and then our brains process and analyze it and formulate our experience. We call that a feeling.[64]

Our emotions are the various states of feeling we experience every day. That means we first need to become more aware of those feelings so we are able to respond to them in an appropriate way. Often, in order to make it through the laundry list of tasks for the day, we ignore our emotions and instead just power through. We put our heads down and just do the work. We push emotions like anger, fear, sadness, excitement, joy, and tenderness out of our minds.

But ignoring our emotions doesn't mean they don't exist.

Thus, the first step in improving our emotional wellness begins with routines of awareness. Rather than moving through our days without taking time to consider our emotions, we intentionally begin to pay more attention to them and how our bodies respond to them, which is crucial to helping increase self-control and related directly to physical wellness and to mindfulness routines. And when we pay more attention to our emotions, we start to recognize how our moods, interactions, and productivity levels change as a result.

We also begin to recognize we are part of a very *human* profession. As we work with other adults or students (or both), we experience a wide swath of emotions throughout the day in ourselves, as well as in our colleagues, students, and families. Emotions such as anger, sadness, fear, joy, tenderness, and excitement all occur naturally based on who we're working with and what we're doing. Our students and colleagues can bring us great joy and hope *and* cause us to feel sad and angry all in the scope of a single day or class period; it's no wonder we're often exhausted!

You can build greater awareness about your daily emotions by pausing to reflect and check in with yourself throughout the day; identify the emotion you're feeling at that given moment. The reflect-and-check question *What emotions am I experiencing right now?* will help you build awareness of what is going on around you, especially when you feel upset and can't quite place your finger on why.

To get started, you can use the following list of several emotions from researcher Brené Brown.[65] Perhaps you can set a few alarms on your phone as a reminder to pause and check in on your current emotional state. You can keep a running record of your emotions, as well as what you were doing and who you were with at the time, to begin building awareness.

Anger	Fear	Judgment
Anxiety	Frustration	Loneliness
Belonging	Gratitude	Love
Blame	Grief	Overwhelm
Curiosity	Guilt	Regret
Disappointment	Happiness	Sadness
Disgust	Humiliation	Shame
Embarrassment	Hurt	Surprise
Empathy	Jealousy	Vulnerability
Excitement	Joy	Worry

You can practice identifying your emotions. Recall the reflect-and-check question *What emotions am I experiencing right now?* Use the list of emotions from Brown and the My Wellness Action space to record your emotions, your feelings, in this moment.

MY WELLNESS ACTION

As you begin to become more aware, you may notice your emotions tend to be more unpleasant than pleasant. Know that you are not alone. In *Permission to Feel: Unlocking the Power of Emotions to Help Our Kids, Ourselves, and Our Society Thrive*, psychologist Marc Brackett shares that in a 2017 study of more than five thousand educators, his team found that most spend nearly 70 percent of their workdays feeling the following emotions: frustration, overwhelm, and stress.[66] Once you are aware of your emotions—recording and noticing patterns around who you're with and what you're doing—you can begin to unpack why you're feeling the way you are; then you are mastering the first routine of the emotional wellness dimension.

Once you've identified what you're feeling, the next awareness step is to notice how you react or respond to your various emotions, with the goal of moving toward reflection before responding, rather than overreacting in the moment. You can include your thoughts, behaviors, language, and body language alongside the emotion you're feeling, who you're with, and what you're doing. Try to do this in real time as much as possible because it's easy to forget the exact emotion and your specific response to that emotion once you've moved too far past the moment. If needed, use video, electronic voice notes, or some other on-the-go format for reflection you can refer to later, when you have quiet time to process.

Keep track of any patterns that begin to emerge around how you tend to respond to strong, unpleasant emotions such as sadness, anger, and fear versus how you typically respond to strong yet pleasant emotions such as happiness, excitement, and tenderness. Pay attention to your interactions with others (both students and colleagues) when you're feeling these strong

Identify your emotions. Label them. Build awareness. Record any emotions you are aware of at this moment in time. Place the day of the week and date by your reflections.

_____

_____

_____

_____

_____

_____

_____

_____

_____

_____

_____

_____

_____

_____

_____

_____

_____

_____

_____

_____

_____

_____

_____

_____

— MY WELLNESS ACTION —

Record the time of day, your emotions, what you were doing, who you were with, and how you responded to those emotions. Use this space to record or keep an electronic record.

Date and day of the week:

Time	My emotion	Event details	Who was there	My response
_____	_____	_____	_____	_____
_____	_____	_____	_____	_____
_____	_____	_____	_____	_____
_____	_____	_____	_____	_____
_____	_____	_____	_____	_____
_____	_____	_____	_____	_____
_____	_____	_____	_____	_____
_____	_____	_____	_____	_____
_____	_____	_____	_____	_____
_____	_____	_____	_____	_____

_____

_____

_____

_____

_____

_____

_____

_____

_____

_____

_____

_____

_____

_____

emotions in order to make connections between how you're feeling and how your emotions impact your relationships.

Dedicate two full days (or maybe a full workweek) to tracking your emotional awareness responses using the My Wellness Action form.

Understanding Routines

Understanding our emotions begins when we uncover the why behind the emotions. When we recognize our emotions and are aware of our responses to them, we can begin understanding what or who evokes pleasant and unpleasant emotions. This is important not because we will be able to avoid these events or people alto-  gether, but because we become aware—forewarned is forearmed. We begin to examine our emotional triggers. Why are we feeling this way?

Re-examine your emotional awareness running record from the My Wellness Action and look for patterns. Do you notice any tendencies?

Perhaps you tend to feel anxious on your way to work, overwhelmed in the afternoon, happy when you're with your fourth-period class, upset when a certain colleague attends a meeting, or deeply grateful on your drive home. Or maybe you start to notice the anxiety that you feel on Monday morning goes away completely by Friday after-noon. Or perhaps your emotions vary widely based on how you slept the night before. Can you begin to connect the dots between your physical wellness routines, mental wellness routines, and your sense of emotional wellness each day?

For this routine, Brackett offers the following questions for consid-eration as you expand your emotional awareness to include reflecting on why you are feeling a certain way.

- What just happened? What was I doing before this happened?

- What might have caused my feelings or reaction?

- What happened this morning, or last night, that might be involved?

- What has happened before with this person that might be connected? (In the event that your emotion has to do with a relationship)

- What memories do I have about this situation or place?[67]

Your emotions provide you with so much information about how you feel. The next natural step, then, is to look for patterns and connect the dots between the emotions you are feeling that day and the events or words that trigger that emotion. Triggers can include observations of unjust treatment; being ignored, excluded, criticized, or helpless; or being wanted, needed, appreciated, and trusted.

Susan David is the author of the *Harvard Business Review*'s Management Idea of the Year and the *Wall Street Journal*'s best-selling book *Emotional Agility: Get Unstuck, Embrace Change, and Thrive in Work and Life*.[68] David notes social psychologist James Pennebaker's work regarding the links between taking the time to write or journal about our emotions and the connections to understanding our emotional processing.

Pennebaker discovered that people who write about intensely emotional experiences have notably increased physical and mental well-being.[69] Over time, those who wrote about their feelings began to understand what those feelings meant, using phrases such as *I have learned*, *It struck me that*, *The reason that*, *I now realize*, and *I understand*. The writing process resulted in the metacognition (awareness and understanding of one's own thought processes) that provided different perspectives on, understandings of, and implications of their emotions more clearly.[70]

You can use your running record to also write about how your emotions manifest in your body physically. Do you feel certain tensions and sensations in your belly or does your heart beat more quickly when you're feeling a certain way? Do you hold tension in your neck or jaw? Is your throat tightening? Where do you notice the physical impact of pleasant emotions versus unpleasant emotions?

Reflect, too, on the intensity and impact of your identified emotions. Are you really angry or just annoyed? Are you ecstatic or just pleased? Are you sad or just disappointed? Think about the word that describes your emotional state and then add two more words next to it that are similar. Which word *best* describes your emotional intensity? Consider assigning your emotion an intensity rating from 1 (low) to 10 (high) to better understand your physical response.

Now, expand your emotional awareness and understanding record to include the intensity of those emotions. Dedicate two full days (or maybe a full workweek) to tracking your emotions and your own understanding of those emotions using a running record for events throughout each day. You can use the My Wellness Action prompt or your own record or journal entries. Be sure to note the intensity of the emotion. Record the time of day, what you were feeling, what you were doing, who you were with, and how intensely you responded to each emotion.

— MY WELLNESS ACTION ——————

Record the time of day and your emotion, and then add notes and reflections about your understanding of any potential event and why you were feeling each emotion. Use this space or keep an electronic or voice record.

Date and day of the week:

Time	My emotion	Event details	The why	The intensity (1–10 scale)
_____	_____	_____	_____	_____
_____	_____	_____	_____	_____
_____	_____	_____	_____	_____
_____	_____	_____	_____	_____
_____	_____	_____	_____	_____
_____	_____	_____	_____	_____
_____	_____	_____	_____	_____
_____	_____	_____	_____	_____
_____	_____	_____	_____	_____
_____	_____	_____	_____	_____

_____

_____

_____

_____

_____

_____

_____

_____

_____

_____

_____

Mindfulness Routines

Now that we've built both awareness and understanding around our emotions, our third routine for emotional wellness improvement is mindfulness. Mindfulness helps us learn how to respond to our emotions and not merely react to them. Mindfulness is an essential tool for staying in control of our emotions. Jon Kabat-Zinn, who coined the phrase, defines mindfulness as "the awareness that emerges through paying attention on purpose, in the present moment, and nonjudgmentally."[71]

Mindfulness is an essential tool for calming ourselves down in order to reach a state of mind where we're able to respond rather than react to our emotions. It can be helpful to think of mindfulness as emotional management. Just as we can work to improve our physical and mental well-being, mindfulness helps us improve our emotional well-being.

Mindfulness routines can take many forms, and it might be helpful to experiment with different strategies to see what feels best for you. Here, we outline three practices to help you get started: (1) mindful breathing, (2) meditating, and (3) journaling.

Mindful Breathing

Mindful breathing is a way to build resilience toward strong, unpleasant feelings such as guilt, anger, frustration, and overwhelm.[72] You can do mindful breathing anywhere and it takes very little time. To get started, simply focus your attention on your breath as you inhale and exhale. It might help to take an exaggerated breath such as this: pause and take a deep inhale through your nose, pause, then deeply exhale through your mouth, pause, and repeat until you start to feel a sense of calm. Note that the emotions may still be present but they should be less intense, and therefore you can improve your response. Try to push your breath into your belly so that your stomach expands on the inhale. If your mind wanders, it's OK. Simply come back to your breath—again and again. Mindful breathing calms our nervous system, reduces stress, increases our alertness, and boosts our immune system.[73]

Meditating

The wildly popular Headspace app tells us about meditation:

> Meditation isn't about becoming a different person, a new person, or even a better person. It's about training in awareness and getting a healthy sense of perspective. You're not trying to turn off your thoughts or feelings.

You're learning to observe them without judgment. And eventually, you may start to better understand them as well.[74]

Similar to mindful breathing, meditation is about focusing on your breath and staying in the present moment. While you can do mindful breathing anytime, anywhere, meditation typically requires a bit more time and focus. To get started, we recommend following a guided meditation. You can find free guided meditations through the UCLA Mindful Awareness Research Center (www.uclahealth.org), and there are many popular apps with free trials, including the aforementioned Headspace (www.headspace.com) and Calm (www. calm.com).

MY WELLNESS ACTION

Journaling

The third practice for developing our mindfulness routines is journaling. This goes back to Pennebaker's research around people who benefit from writing about intense experiences.[75] Mindful website senior editor Amber Tucker explains that "writing mindfully can loosen the grip of sticky emotions by bringing them out of the dark. With just a pen and paper, or an app, we can create the habit of being there for ourselves."[76] To engage in journaling as a mindfulness practice, you simply need to write. There's no right or wrong way to do this.

As you've been keeping a running record of your emotions in the My Wellness Actions (pages 49, 50, and 53), you've already begun to experiment with journaling. To expand on this, you might simply engage in a brain dump where you get your thoughts out of your mind and onto the paper, without worrying about editing yourself or feeling compelled to be neat, organized, or thorough. Or you can simply take a moment to check in with yourself via writing. Doodling or coloring, especially to express your emotions, are other ways to journal without having to write words.[77] When you're journaling, don't worry about spelling or grammar. Simply get your thoughts and feelings out of your head and down on paper. The benefit is that

Which one of these three mindfulness routine suggestions—(1) mindful breathing, (2) meditating, or (3) journaling—will you commit to trying this week? Write about how you will take and sustain this mindfulness action.

_____

_____

_____

_____

_____

_____

_____

_____

_____

_____

_____

_____

_____

_____

_____

_____

_____

_____

_____

_____

_____

you can let your emotions go and begin to feel lighter simply by writing them down.

Emotional Wellness: Our Stories

Each dimension of wellness for educators tells a story about the ebb and flow for living our best lives. In this section of the chapter, we (Tina and Tim) briefly share some of our wellness stories and then invite you to write and share your wellness journey, too.

Tina's Story

Emotional wellness is something I recommit to every single day. I'd much rather stuff my emotions down and ignore them than deal with them because, well, *I have too much to do right now* to think about my feelings. Of course, I know that's simply a recipe for disaster. Pretending everything's fine when it's not and plowing through the day without ever stopping to consider what I'm feeling and why is not healthy. In the past, ignoring my emotions led to weight gain, sleepless nights, and strained relationships. In fact, it's also what leads to burnout and exhaustion—stages I've definitely touched at various points in my career.

I've purposefully built mindfulness practices into my day in order to force myself to take stock of my emotions, understand where those feelings are coming from, and attend to them in healthy ways. For example, I begin each day with a two-minute meditation followed by a few pages of journaling. Throughout the day, I pause to take three breaths (I always place one hand on my belly while I do this to remind myself to take a deep breath, or *belly breath*) and check in with myself to determine how I'm feeling and what I might need in that moment.[78] At the end of the day, I do a relaxing meditation to lull me to sleep.

And it all works. It really does.

I'm significantly calmer, better equipped to handle unexpected challenges that come my way, and more aware of how my emotions impact those around me (and vice versa). I'm able to connect my emotional wellness to my physical, mental, and social wellness, and I continue to find new patterns and connect more dots between the emotions I'm currently feeling, why I'm feeling the way I do, and how I can have a healthy response to those emotions. I'm also at a healthier weight, am able to sleep better, and have stronger relationships with those I'm closest to.

Tim's Story

My entire teaching career, I have always embraced my emotions. My feelings and the feelings of others have mattered deeply. A lot. I don't really know why. I think it is just part of my hard and soft wiring as a teacher.

The challenge for me has been to embrace a journey of emotional *wellness*. How can I respond to those feelings in a way that benefits my overall physical, mental, emotional, and social well-being? Surprisingly, it took me a long time to get there. I was roughly in my twentieth season of teaching before I saw the benefits to practicing mindfulness routines.

I am somewhat of a linear thinker. You know: step one, step two, and so on. When I am upset about a current event in my life, sometimes I can get stuck—not quite able to figure out what is bothering me. Bothering me so much, it can interfere with my daily life routines. In the beginning, I was amazed at how well the following mindfulness routine would work for me when I was stuck.

I would grab a notepad and do the following.

1. Identify which of these six emotions I was feeling right then: (1) sad, (2) angry, (3) scared, (4) happy, (5) excited, or (6) tender (SASHET).[79]

2. Ask why I was feeling this way.

3. Write about the entire scenario or situation and all of *my* feelings about why I was feeling anxious or upset.

This new routine almost always diminished the strength or intensity of the (usually unpleasant) emotion I was feeling, provided greater clarity to the parts of the experience that were about me or others, dissipated my angst, and allowed me to respond to my life experiences in a way that was consistent and more stable for others.

It is hard to be around colleagues who exhibit emotional responses that are unhealthy for others. I wanted to make sure those around me could be confident that on most days, I would respond in a way that was emotionally safe for them and for me.

These days, I also use a mental check-in with my emotions. As a runner, running provides an easy place and space for me to let my mind decompress and then process my emotions of the day. Or better yet, help me to understand how to have a more positive response to others when certain emotions rise up, as they always do.

To go deeper into this thinking and watch us (Tina and Tim) in conversation about this dimension of educator wellness, scan the QR code using your smartphone or device, or visit **go.SolutionTree.com/educatorwellness** to access the URLs for all videos.

Emotional Wellness
www.SolutionTree.com/EmotionalWellness

Summarizing Thoughts

Working on our emotional wellness and avoiding the frustration of getting stuck in negative judgments around our sadness, anger, or fear is a daily uphill climb. It is hard work to resist the tendency to just bury our emotions and not reveal to ourselves, much less to others, how we *really* feel today. Learning how to respond to our emotions (rather than react) will serve us well as educators. Our students (and our colleagues) need us to be in a positive emotional state every day. Their cognition and learning depend on it.

Remember these five core takeaways regarding your daily emotional wellness routines.

1. Become emotionally aware.
2. Understand your emotional why.
3. Respond—don't react—to your daily emotions.
4. Practice mindfulness.
5. Remember that your emotions impact student cognition.

Seek emotional awareness every day, strive to understand the emotional triggers that can cause an unhealthy reaction to an event or a person, and practice mindfulness routines that allow you to respond rather than react. And as always, give yourself grace as you maneuver through this work; it's not easy, but it is important.

Now it is your turn!

Emotional Wellness: Your Story

Our emotions are a part of our everyday lives and impact our work and our relationships. We build awareness around our emotions, strive to understand them better, and then respond in ways that are healthy for us, our students, and our colleagues. You have read this chapter, answered the prompts, and considered parts of our (Tim and Tina's) stories, based on our experiences.

Take some time to write about your personal emotional wellness story. Don't worry if you don't consider yourself a writer. This isn't about the writing; it's about the reflection. You can use the prompts we provide or simply write your own story and next steps for improving the emotional wellness dimension in your professional life! Consider placing a date and time by each entry as you tell your wellness story, and reference figure B.3 (page 86) as needed.

What story of hope for your emotional wellness future do you want to write to yourself or perhaps share with a trusted other?

_____

_____

_____

_____

_____

_____

_____

_____

_____

_____

_____

_____

_____

_____

_____

_____

_____

_____

_____

Examine the list of summarizing thoughts (page 58). Of the five ideas listed, which one needs to be a focus of action for you in the next few months? Write out two *I will* statements to help ensure your growth in the emotional wellness dimension of your work life.

_____

_____

_____

_____

_____

_____

_____

_____

_____

_____

_____

_____

_____

_____

_____

_____

_____

_____

_____

_____

_____

_____

Consider current progress in your physical and mental wellness dimensions from chapters 1 (page 8) and 2 (page 24). How is progress in your food, movement, and sleep routines, or in your decision, balance, and efficacy routines impacting your positive emotional wellness this week?

_____

_____

_____

_____

_____

_____

_____

_____

_____

_____

_____

_____

_____

_____

_____

_____

_____

_____

_____

_____

_____

_____

_____

_____

_____

_____

_____

_____

Minor changes in your mindfulness routines will add up quickly and impact your relational awareness and understanding of others. Be patient with your progress and know there will be a positive impact on your social wellness too. And that educator wellness dimension is next!

CHAPTER 4
The Social Wellness Dimension

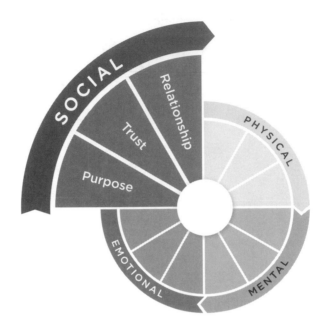

I beg of you to remember that wherever our life touches yours, we help or hinder. Wherever your life touches ours, you make us stronger or weaker.

—Booker T. Washington

We are wired to connect.

Evolutionary biologists and behavioral psychologists have found neural and, in some cases, genetic evidence of a predisposition to connect with colleagues. Professor of entrepreneurial legal studies at Harvard Law School Yochai Benkler indicates, "We are more cooperative and less selfish than most people believe."[80]

We participate every day in social wellness routines with our colleagues, students, friends, and family members. Goleman describes how "our social interactions play a role in reshaping our brain, through *neuroplasticity*, which means that repeated experiences [with others] sculpt the shape, size, and number of neurons and their synaptic connections."[81] Goleman defines our *social intelligence* as a "shorthand term for being intelligent not just *about* our relationships, but also *in* them."[82] Much of our success as educators depends on our ability to be socially intelligent about our relationships with others!

In chapters 1 through 3, we examined the first three dimensions of our wellness—(1) physical, (2) mental, and (3) emotional. Those routines exposed interconnected wellness routines for your more *individual* well-being and improvement. Those chapters included routines about our self-care, self-regulation, self-awareness, self-understanding, self-efficacy, and self-responsibility. And now, in this chapter, the social wellness dimension of the Wellness Solutions for Educators framework (page 81), we explore routines for expanding our relationships with others, building trust, and connecting to our purpose.

Through our social wellness progress, we maintain meaningful friendships, experience more trusting relationships, develop more positive professional connections, and deliver on the promise of our primary purpose as educators: to serve the growth and successful learning of our students and colleagues.

Imagine going for a walk with your best friend as you discuss your feelings about the day's decisions, stresses, and challenges. In one thirty-minute walk, you have hit on a trifecta of educator wellness routines: physical (you're walking), mental (you're reflecting and sharing), and emotional (you're feeling). Yet that walk was not alone. It was filled with more than just the self-talk voice in your head. There was the additional dance of the social experience, the social give and take, the mutual nourishing of your relationship with that friend.

We need positive social connection to thrive in our first three dimensions of wellness. Our social wellness serves our physical, mental, and emotional wellness and vice versa. Students, colleagues, friends, and

family members are more likely to desire social connection with us when we are in a positive emotional response space as well. Consider this observation from Gupta:

> Staying social and interacting with others in meaningful ways can provide a buffer against the harmful effects of stress on the brain. People with *fewer* social connections have disrupted sleep patterns, altered immune systems, more inflammation, and higher levels of stress hormones.[83]

Thus, we should pay attention to our relationship routines as much as we do our physical wellness routines. That trifecta walk with your friend is actually a superfecta! Besides the physical, mental, and emotional benefits already highlighted, there's also the social benefit that comes from connection. Warm connections are a core feature of our optimal human experiences.

Relationship Routines

Imagine delaying or preventing your physical and mental decline. If you would like to, then consider the factors that have an impact on this desired delay: your intelligence quotient (IQ), your money, your fame, your social class, your hard work, your genes, and your relationships. Which of these factors would you rank most important to preventing this decline?

If you said your relationships, you are correct.

There is a substantial benefit when you are able to develop healthy relationships both at home with your family and friends and at work with your students and colleagues. Consider the ongoing eighty-year-long Harvard Study of Adult Development:

> "The surprising finding is that our relationships and how happy we are in our relationships has a powerful influence on our health," said Robert Waldinger, director of the study, a psychiatrist at Massachusetts General Hospital and a professor of psychiatry at Harvard Medical School. "Taking care of your body is important, but tending to your relationships is a form of self-care too . . ."

> Close relationships, more than money or fame, are what keep people happy throughout their lives. . . . Those ties protect people from life's discontents, help to delay mental and physical decline, and are better predictors of long and happy lives than social class, IQ, or even genes.[84]

We are happier in our personal and our professional lives when we work together, lean into, and build bonds with family members and friends and develop positive working relationships with students and colleagues. As we examine this first routine for social wellness, the *quality* of our close relationships is what really matters.

Susan Moore Johnson of the Harvard Graduate School of Education, in her 2019 book *Where Teachers Thrive: Organizing Schools for Success*, describes professional working conditions that attract and enable teachers to continuously improve their craft: "In well-organized schools, teachers constantly work with and learn from each other. Those schools are designed to build the collective capacity of all teachers to ensure that students receive consistently good or great instruction."[85]

Yet, Johnson goes on to say, the "more that teachers—even the best among them—keep to themselves, the more the content and quality of instruction varies from classroom to classroom . . . students are very likely to get an uneven and incoherent education."[86] If we understand the equity benefits for students, our moral responsibly to do good and not harm, and the social wellness benefits of working together, why is it so many in our profession choose to work in isolation?

When our relationships at work become a priority every day, we move the needle on being *in* relationship with others by paying attention to others. In turn, our individual self-efficacy is enhanced because we work well in deep relationship toward the development of our collective teams' efficacy—a type of group confidence and competence builder we experience as we dissolve barriers to student learning by working as a team, together.[87]

From best-selling researcher and author Rath:

> The single greatest driver of both achievement and well-being is understanding how your daily efforts enhance the lives of others. Scientists have determined that we as human beings are innately other directed—connecting and contributing to something beyond the self.[88]

The question, of course, is, Do your students and colleagues feel as if their relationship with you will be mutually nourishing? Is *What do my students or colleagues need from me?* an important question for you?

Examine the following four criteria from author Douglas Reeves and his interpretation regarding the work of Daniel Goleman for improving your relationship-building and sense-of-belonging routines.[89] Consider asking a trusted colleague to tell you which one he or she thinks you are especially good with and which one you might need to spend more time working on and see if it matches with your own thinking.

1. *Listen without interruption or judgment.* Pay attention to or perhaps even record your next discussion with a colleague or at your teacher team meeting, or even just listen in on a conversation that's being held nearby. Reflect on how often you interrupt others when they are speaking and how often you are interrupted by others. If you are listening in on a conversation, observe how often each person interrupts the other. (Hint: It will be more often than you believe.)

2. *Practice empathy by asking questions.* How often do you "seek first to understand the meaning and intent of the words of others" and not assume you know what they mean?[90] How often do you say, "Tell me more" or "How could I support you in this work?" or "Why do you believe that is an important issue?" Do you seek to understand the subtle intention of others?

3. *Never betray a private conversation.*[91] Is the fine line between what is for public knowledge and what is private knowledge crystal clear to you and to the members of your team? How well do you respect the confidences of your conversations with others? Do you have a clear understanding of what has been decided versus merely discussed by your team, and do you ask when it is best to share those decisions with others? Do you ask for permission before sharing an email, text, or in-person conversation detail with others?

4. *Exhibit genuine passion and compassion for others.* How well do you exhibit genuine interest and pay attention to your colleagues' physical, mental, and emotional well-being needs? Do you take action as needed to know and support your colleagues and friends? Do you know their birthdays or the names of their children or significant others? Do you create energy that benefits your students and colleagues?

By choosing to invest time in others, maximizing your strengths to benefit one another, and refusing to let each other quit the hard work of student success as part of your daily mission, you begin to experience intimacy in your work life, and neglect is cast aside. Mutually nourishing relationships can become the norm.

Research demonstrates the link between positive social relationships at work and lower burnout rates, increased work satisfaction, and improved productivity.[92] We feel our best when our relationships are positive. There is a sense of satisfaction, safety, and comfort in our work. Stanford psychologist Emma Seppälä indicates the outcome of becoming more socially connected is an increase in our mental well-being and self-esteem.[93] Thus, our road to social wellness runs through our willingness to create a culture of belonging and inclusion with each of our students and colleagues.

To build relationship routines that nurture inclusion and belonging at your team meetings or in your office space, consider these ten strategies and norms. Consider asking your team members (as well as yourself) to rate their effectiveness toward adhering to these relationship-building norms.

1. Make it safe to speak up by listening without judgment.

2. Listen to the voices of others and do not interrupt.

3. Prod yourself to speak up if you tend to be quiet.

4. Slow down the voices of those who want to talk first.

5. Advocate your position or ideas, and then ask for suggestions to improve them.

6. Gracefully address any ego-driven behaviors in the group.

7. Sharpen the focus of your purpose: improved student learning.

8. Brainstorm new ideas for improved student learning and experiment together.

9. Commit to work and fun. Say *thank you* a lot.

10. Celebrate, celebrate, celebrate. Every week.

Examine this list of relationship-building norms for your team meetings. Then answer the My Wellness Action prompt.

MY WELLNESS ACTION

Name two relational norms that are strengths and name two norms that need improvement. Then write out two I will actions you need to take in order to improve your relationship building.

_____

_____

_____

_____

_____

_____

_____

_____

_____

_____

_____

_____

_____

_____

_____

_____

_____

_____

_____

_____

_____

_____

Trust Routines

Grab a pen and pad of paper (digital or otherwise) or just use the margins of this guidebook to answer the following two prompts before you read further. We will come back to your answers later.

1. Write the names of two people in your professional life whom you trust deeply.

2. For each, write three descriptive one-word characteristics of that person.

Improving our social wellness partially resides in improving our routines for trust in our relationships and connections with others; and there are a lot of benefits. Paul J. Zak is the founding director of the Center for Neuroeconomics Studies and a professor of economics, psychology, and management at Claremont Graduate University. Zak indicates that employees in high-trust organizations collaborate better, suffer less prolonged stress, and in general experience greater happiness.[94]

Trust, as a routine you practice, is the "assured reliance on the character, ability, strength, or truth of someone."[95] And, trust is a mutually nourishing two-way street.

Our trust routines are part of a dynamic process with others that requires a sustained willingness to demonstrate vulnerability and respect for our professional relationships. In *Daring Greatly: How the Courage to Be Vulnerable Transforms the Way We Live, Love, Parent, and Lead*, Brown describes vulnerability as "uncertainty, risk and emotional exposure."[96]

So, consider this question: Based on your professional experiences, which comes first—vulnerability or trust? If you are more vulnerable with your colleagues, does that build trust? Or does trust build into and shape your willingness to be vulnerable?

What is your intuitive guess? And why?

It turns out, vulnerability is *the* pathway to trusting others.

Surprisingly, perhaps, the neuroscience of trust affirms vulnerability as a precursor to trust.[97] Vulnerability creates and strengthens a trust culture throughout your team, classroom, school, or district. As vulnerability becomes a core value of your school's culture, you are more likely to view asking for help as a strength of your work life, and less as a weakness.

Zak verifies one of the primary methods for building team trust is to demonstrate vulnerability with your colleagues:

> Leaders in high-trust workplaces ask for help from colleagues instead of just telling them to do things. My research team has found that this stimulates oxytocin production in others, increasing their trust and cooperation. Asking for help is a sign of a secure leader [think educator]—one who engages everyone to reach goals . . . Asking for help is effective because it taps into the natural human impulse to cooperate with others.[98]

So, vulnerability is your willingness, despite your confidence in your capabilities, to admit you don't know everything. You actively seek help from others as you grow your sense of self-efficacy discussed as part of your mental wellness improvement in chapter 2 (page 24). You might ask a colleague to join your daily walk in order to help you stay accountable to your movement routine goals from chapter 1 (page 8), or ask a colleague about how to become more aware of your emotional responses (chapter 3, page 44) during more stressful situations.

We develop routines for vulnerability when both the giver (I'll signal my vulnerability to you) and the receiver (you'll hopefully accept, instead of reject, my request for help) interact in a communication dance together.

Our back-and-forth communication signals our vulnerability to one another, and we, in turn, build a more trusting relationship per author Daniel Coyle: "Vulnerability is less about the sender than the receiver."[99] Coyle then quotes professor Jeffrey T. Polzer: "The second person is the key."[100] According to research by Harry T. Reis and colleagues, being responsive to the other person's vulnerability is important for the sustained quality of close relationships.[101]

Thus, trust is earned through our intentional choice to be vulnerable with one another, developed through our actions that are real and genuine, and then improved through our willingness to respond and listen in ways that are safe, supportive, and without judgment. This is a socially mature pathway.

Trust occurs as you ensure students and colleagues feel respected *without being judged*. What could be better than an environment of trust in which students and colleagues alike feel strong, know who they are, feel as if they are listened to, and know how they can contribute?

Marissa King is a professor of organizational behavior at the Yale School of Management. In her book *Social Chemistry: Decoding the*

After deeply listening to your friend or colleague without interruption, write about what you learned from the experience and how it felt to listen without judgment.

_____
_____
_____
_____
_____
_____
_____
_____
_____
_____
_____
_____
_____
_____
_____
_____
_____
_____
_____
_____
_____
_____
_____

Patterns of Human Connection, King describes three essential components in the field of listening research.[102]

1. A cognitive component: Do you remember and understand what you hear?

2. A behavioral component: Do you make eye contact, smile, and nod?

3. An affective or ethical component: Are you listening *without* judgment?

King points out that less than 2 percent of the population has had any organized listening training, and that the training is, for the most part, in regard to the cognitive and behavioral components only: "But listening is about more than comprehending words. It is about suspending judgment."[103] This is a type of deep listening that represents a process of listening *to learn*.

King's suggestion is to:

> Find a friend or colleague and take two minutes to listen to him or her respond to the simple question, 'What is it like to be you today?' without any form of interruption. Don't ask questions, or provide advice or affirmations, just listen.[104]

MY WELLNESS ACTION

The routine of deep listening without judgment illuminates our compassion, our connections, and our common humanity. It "is the kind of listening that can help relieve the suffering of another person. You listen with only one purpose: to help him or her empty his heart."[105] Trust gradually develops once any judgment from the listener is cast aside.

Remember our request at the opening of this section where we asked you to name two colleagues you trust with three corresponding characteristics (page 68)? What were the words you used? That question was part of a Gallup poll.[106] When asked what trust meant, the respondents indicated honesty, integrity, and respect. Honesty and integrity are our willingness to be vulnerable, to ask for help as a strength and not a weakness, to speak with truth, to align our actions with our responsibility for promoting good in others, and to listen to our students and colleagues without judgment—all trust-building routines. Routines that encourage others to socialize with us in a mutually nourishing way.

Purpose Routines

Because we work in a profession that thrives in our stewardship of the social and emotional welfare of others—our students and colleagues—our profession expects a lot from us. It expects us to bring our best selves forward to each day.

Our profession is a tough job.

And it is not for everyone.

If you are reading this guidebook and have made it to this twelfth and final wellness routine, you understand how all of our wellness actions and routines thus far are mostly for the very singular purpose of helping us meet our purpose as educators and to help overcome the adversity we often face. We wish to avoid the prolonged stress, mental and physical exhaustion, and emotional toll the education profession can take on our overall well-being. And staying close to knowing our why—why we joined *this* profession—serves our wellness along the way. Whether you are two or twenty seasons into your professional career as an educator, you most likely have had someone outside of education ask you your *why*.

Why do you do it? *Why* do you call yourself teacher and leader? *Why* did you become an educator, and *why* are you part of the educational enterprise?

From the relentless details of the daily grind to the extreme complexities of teaching and leading during great adversity (such as the COVID-19 pandemic), why? And the best explanation we can give is this: *Somehow, deep in the recesses of our brains, we chose education for our life's work because we had to. Teaching and leading others is just who we are.*

Throwing your whole self into this work fulfills your purpose in life and gives your voice a place to sing. You understand that your profession will include difficult moments in time—where the costs of this choice for your life's work will outweigh the benefits. And yet, you also know there is no doubt in your mind. Teaching and leading, educating others, is who you are; it is your identity. And knowing this truth is the start of your purpose-building routine.

Parker J. Palmer is the founder and senior partner emeritus for the Center for Courage and Renewal. In his book *Let Your Life Speak: Listening for the Voice of Vocation*, he provides wise insight into our purpose-building routines:

> I must listen to my life and try to understand what it is truly about—quite apart from what I would like it to be about— or my life will never represent anything real in the world, no matter how earnest my intentions.
>
> That insight is hidden in the word *vocation* itself, which is rooted in the Latin for "voice." Vocation does not mean a goal that I pursue. It means a calling that I hear. Before I can tell my life what I want to do with it, I must listen to my life telling me who I am. I must listen for the truths and the values at the heart of my own identity, not the standards by which I *must* live—but the standards by which I cannot help but live if I am living my own life.[107]

Author David Brooks shares insight into why we stand up through the storms of well-being we must weather:

> Vocations invariably have testing periods—periods where the costs outweigh the benefits. If you were driven by a career mentality you would quit. You're putting more into this thing than you are getting out. But a person who has found a vocation doesn't really feel she has a choice. It would be a violation of her own nature.[108]

Our social wellness pursuit begins to reveal the truth about our professional life's meaning and purpose. We discover once again the power of our chosen profession. In the words of Booker T. Washington, "I beg of you to remember that wherever our life touches yours, we help or hinder. Wherever your life touches ours, you make us stronger or weaker."[109] There is something spiritual and deep in knowing the power we possess to help and not hinder others. To make others stronger and more confident and more capable, and not weaker.

That is a lot of responsibility. Sometimes, you can feel the weight of choosing to become an educator. We steward the success of every child or teenager entrusted to us. There is a lot at stake. Our students, our children, are depending on us. They are depending on our wellness. Which is why this final routine of connecting to our purpose is achieved by participating in each of the other eleven wellness routines discussed in this guidebook. We pursue our wellness as educators because it allows us to live our best lives each day in a profession that serves our greater purpose in life.

Your physical wellness routines of food, movement, and sleep are each designed to keep you living in a space where physically you can serve the purpose of your work with a relentless energy and enthusiasm day after day.

Your mental wellness routines for wise and efficient decision making, daily moments of quiet and solitude for a well-balanced and brain-refreshed life, and the continuous improvement of your self-efficacy keep you confident, humble, and seeking to improve because you know our profession serves your purpose in the journey of serving others, and you can feel that joy even on the worst of days.

Your emotional wellness is a long journey through awareness to understanding, to the maturity of mindfulness, where mindful breathing, meditating, and journaling are examples of purpose-connecting routines.

In this final chapter, relationship and trust routines, rooted in improving the quality of our connections with others, are exactly the point. We serve our purpose as educators by understanding we exist to build high-quality, incredible relationships with others.

Wellness expert Deepak Chopra leaves us with one last purpose-building routine.[110] Try it if you like. See how it feels and fits for you.

Keep your feet firmly planted on the ground.

Keep your hands open.

Observe your breath. As you observe your breath, thought also settles.

And now bring your awareness to your heart.

> Question number one: Who am I? Just be aware of any sensations, images, feelings, or thoughts that spontaneously come to you.
>
> Question number two: What is my deepest desire? What do I want? [Allow] any sensation, image, feeling, or thought to come to you.
>
> Third question: What is my purpose? What is my calling? Allowing any sensation, image, feeling, or thought to come to you.
>
> Final question: What am I grateful for? Allowing any sensation, image, feeling, or thought to come to you. Gratitude will open the door to you, to your soul.[111]

Social Wellness: Our Stories

Each dimension of wellness for educators tells a story about the ebb and flow for living our best lives. In this section of the chapter, we (Tina and Tim) briefly share some of our wellness stories and then invite you to write and share your wellness journey, too.

Tim's Story

My first thought is that my social wellness routines are part of a never-ending and elusive process for my continual improvement. My second thought is how often I feel as if I am failing to connect deeply with all of my personal and professional relationships. Sometimes I take my family and close colleague relationships for granted. They know I care for them and love them; do I really need to pay attention to them every day? The answer is yes.

I also feel a daily pressure to respond, in an era of social media. Failure to text, email, Instagram, Facebook post, or tweet in a timely manner can cause others to think you don't like them, or you are in a bad mood, or worse, they are not important to you. And timeliness is defined within a wide variance, depending on the family member or professional colleague. In some ways, I think we use timeliness of response as a weapon to signal who and what is really important in our lives. Or perhaps to show our indifference.

And yet our social wellness is the glue that unites us in our work and fuels our purpose. We are in a relationship-driven profession. And I love it! Teaching has served my purpose in life, and I am grateful. I love the energy and feeling of family with my students and colleagues. We are expected to help others feel connected and included as part of the learning process, *and* we are to be intentional about listening to and noticing others—every day.

Early in my career as an educator, I began a simple routine of thinking about two students or colleagues I had not connected with lately. I would get quiet on my way home from work each day, and just think about two names and faces that would come to mind. Before I went to bed, I would write those two students or colleagues a note of appreciation on a five-by-seven notecard. A quiet, non-public celebration of their actions and effort. Occasionally, I would write that note to myself or to a family member. These days I write these notes in an email or text.

Every day. Three-hundred-sixty-five days a year. For forty-seven years. That is 34,000-plus (I missed a few days) notes. My way of connecting. My way of saying *you belong*. My way of letting you know what you have taught me or how much I respect your contributions to others—your students especially, but your colleagues, too. It may not seem like much. I doubt very few of my colleagues from thirty years ago remember much about working with me, but just maybe there is a five-by-seven notecard stuck somewhere in a shoebox that reminds them of how much joy we had working together on behalf of our students. Always signed by me, and always with a smiley face.

Tina's Story

It can feel like our phones have become attached to our bodies. It can feel like the magic of conversation is becoming a bit of a lost art. We've all had the unpleasant experience where we're talking with someone else and suddenly he or she loses eye contact with us and instead focuses on his or her phone (despite nodding and telling us, "Keep going, I'm still listening; I just need to respond to this text really quick"). It's the worst. Personally, that simple act makes me feel deflated and uninteresting, and I typically find myself shutting down while I begin to fidget awkwardly. As much as I loathe this feeling from the receiving end, I know I'm guilty of doing it to others, too.

I'm working on it, though.

One of the great lessons of the COVID-19 pandemic was the importance of face-to-face human connection. I no longer take in-person time with family, friends, and colleagues for granted. Instead, I am grateful to soak up every moment we have together. As a way to express my gratitude for this time, I'm purposeful in putting my phone on Do Not Disturb and either tucking it away or turning it facedown so that I'm not drawn to it.

I also have a renewed commitment to being genuinely curious and engaging in deep listening when I'm face to face with people I care about. I love to tell stories, and so I have to really work on resisting the urge to plow over someone else's story with my own, and instead focus on the gift that is provided when we are beautiful listeners.

As simple as *deep listening* sounds, I've found that it actually takes deliberate practice. I often slip into old patterns where I talk way more than I listen and I spend more time thinking about what I'm going to say next than I do simply soaking up what I'm hearing. But when I am intentional about prioritizing my social wellness through the art of listening, I feel a greater sense of calm and a deep connection with the person I'm engaging in conversation with; it's such a glorious gift.

To go deeper into this thinking and watch us (Tina and Tim) in conversation about this dimension of educator wellness, scan the QR code using your smartphone or device, or visit **go.SolutionTree.com/educatorwellness** to access the URLs for all videos.

Social Wellness
www.SolutionTree.com/SocialWellness

Summarizing Thoughts

Becoming intentional about our social wellness and developing improved relational skills and routines are at the very heart of our desired impact as educators. Social wellness requires reaching out to others in such a way they will want to reach out to us. It is hard work to build intentional and trustworthy relationships through a commitment to vulnerability and strong humility. Ultimately, our professional lives thrive when filled with defining moments that remind us of our fundamental purpose as educators: to make a difference in this world by educating the next generation well through our deep love and compassion for others.

Remember these five core takeaways regarding your daily social wellness routines.

1. We are wired to connect with others.

2. Positive relationships predict success in life.

3. Vulnerability precedes trust.

4. Practice deep listening without judging others.

5. Keep your purpose close. You'll need it!

We invite you to consider this advice: seek to be socially intelligent and aware every day. Seek to bring your best self to your work life each day. Your students and colleagues are counting on it! Seek to trust others by being vulnerable. Seek to remember and reconnect to your purpose from time to time.

Now it is your turn!

Social Wellness: Your Story

Our professional life thrives when we reflect on and work to gradually improve our routines for social wellness. Our relationships with others are at the heart of our everyday teaching and leading life. We can measure our social wellness progress based on the three routines of building (1) relationships, (2) trust, and (3) purpose as we become more socially intelligent, become more vulnerable with others, and stay connected to our purpose as educators.

Take some time to write about your personal social wellness story. Don't worry if you don't consider yourself a writer. This isn't about the writing; it's about the reflection. You can use the prompts we provide or simply write your own story and next steps for improving the social wellness dimension in your professional life!

How has this chapter connected to your daily experiences with others? What is the story of hope and purpose you want to write to yourself or perhaps share with others? How do you develop an awareness of your purpose and then respond in ways that are healthy for you and all of those around you? Tell your story and use as much space as you need. Consider placing a date and time by each entry as you tell your wellness story, and reference figure B.4 (page 87) as needed.

What is the story of hope for the social wellness future you want to write to yourself or perhaps share with a trusted other?

_____

_____

_____

_____

_____

_____

_____

_____

_____

_____

_____

_____

_____

_____

_____

_____

_____

_____

_____

_____

_____

_____

Examine the list of summarizing thoughts (page 76). Of the five ideas listed, which one needs to be a focus of action for you in the next few months? Write out two *I will* statements to help ensure your growth in this social dimension of your work life.

_____

_____

_____

_____

_____

_____

_____

_____

_____

_____

_____

_____

_____

_____

_____

_____

_____

_____

_____

_____

_____

_____

Consider your current progress in your social wellness routines. How is progress (or lack of progress—which happens) in your physical, mental, and emotional wellness dimensions being served by your improved relationships with others and greater connection to your purpose as an educator?

_____

_____

_____

_____

_____

_____

_____

_____

_____

_____

_____

_____

_____

_____

_____

_____

_____

_____

_____

_____

_____

_____

_____

_____

_____

_____

_____

In the end, always remember to connect to your why on your most difficult days. *Listen without judgment* is the best advice you can model and mentor. So remember, as Washington said, "Wherever our life touches yours, we help or hinder. Wherever your life touches ours, you make us stronger or weaker."[112] Above all, let your life speak with grace, joy, gratitude, and demonstrations of educator wellness for yourself and others.

Wellness Solutions for Educators *Framework*

Educator wellness is an active process toward achieving a positive state of good health and enhanced physical, mental, emotional, and social well-being, as a lifelong professional goal. See figure A.1.

Physical Wellness Dimension	**Food Routines** Consider what and when you eat and drink and how well you hydrate during the day.	**Movement Routines** Consider what, when, and how well you move during the day.	**Sleep Routines** Consider how much sleep and rest you get during each twenty-four-hour cycle.
Mental Wellness Dimension	**Decision Routines** Consider how well you reduce, automate, and regulate the decisions you make each day to avoid decision fatigue.	**Balance Routines** Consider how well you live a busy, high-energy, well-balanced day-to-day work life and avoid prolonged stress.	**Efficacy Routines** Consider how well you build your confidence and competence and improve your work-life capabilities each day.
Emotional Wellness Dimension	**Awareness Routines** Consider how well you identify, keep track of, and respond to your daily emotions.	**Understanding Routines** Consider the why behind your emotions and how well you reflect on your responses to different emotions.	**Mindfulness Routines** Consider how well you use mindfulness practices to respond rather than react to your strong and more unpleasant emotions.
Social Wellness Dimension	**Relationship Routines** Consider how well you and your colleagues build strong relationships and social connections together.	**Trust Routines** Consider how well you build daily work-life routines of vulnerability and deep listening without judgment of others.	**Purpose Routines** Consider how your daily work life feeds into your greater purpose and helps you find meaning and joy in your work life.

Figure A.1: Wellness Solutions for Educators framework—Dimensions and routines.

Visit **go.SolutionTree.com/educatorwellness** for a free reproducible version of this figure.

APPENDIX B

Wellness Solutions for Educators
Rating, Reflecting, Goal Setting, Planning, and Progress Monitoring Protocol

Here is a guide for how to use the eight figures and two parts of appendix B: *Rating, Reflecting, Goal Setting, Planning, and Progress Monitoring* protocol.

Part I: Rating and Reflecting—Figures B.1–B.4

This section of the protocol asks you to rate and reflect on your current state of well-being and wellness for each of the four dimensions and three corresponding routines discussed in the book and listed as part of the Wellness Solutions for Educators framework.

Figure B.1: Educator wellness self-rating and reflection—*Physical wellness routines.*

Figure B.2: Educator wellness self-rating and reflection—*Mental wellness routines.*

Figure B.3: Educator wellness self-rating and reflection—*Emotional wellness routines.*

Figure B.4: Educator wellness self-rating and reflection—*Social wellness routines.*

You will notice each figure represents one wellness dimension and its three corresponding routines, followed by six yes or no action statements for each routine.

Use the following process to complete each rating and reflecting protocol provided in figures B.1–B.4.

1. Read the six yes or no action statements for each routine. Check the box if your response is yes; leave the box blank if your response is no.

2. For each routine, give yourself a rating score between 1–4 in the space provided. You can use a marker or a pen to highlight your score.

3. Use the bottom space of figures B.1–B.4 to identify your strongest routine for that corresponding dimension and to identify your wellness routine most in need of improvement. Use the space to briefly comment your reflection.

Part II: Planning, Goal Setting, and Progress Monitoring—Figures B.5–B.8

This section of appendix B asks you to plan for strategies and actions using figures B.5 and B.6 and then use the progress monitoring tools provided in figures B.7 and B.8 to measure your ongoing wellness improvement. You can use figures B.5–B.8 to help you meet goals for wellness proficiency (ratings of 3.5 or higher) with each routine you identified for improvement.

Figure B.5: Educator wellness planning tool—Routines that are strengths.

Figure B.6: Educator wellness planning tool—Routines for improvement.

Figures B.5 and B.6 are planning tools with which you identify specific strategies and actions. In figure B.5, you write about strategies you use for the routines that represent areas of strength for you. Write *I do . . .* statements as you consider why you are successful for the identified routine. In figure B.6, you write about strategies and actions you need to take to become more proficient in each identified routine. You write these statements as actions, starting with *I will . . . .*

Figure B.7: Educator wellness goal setting and progress monitoring tool—*Physical and mental wellness progress monitoring.*

Figure B.8: Educator wellness goal setting and progress monitoring tool—*Emotional and social wellness progress monitoring.*

Use figures B.7 and B.8 as progress monitoring tools for each dimension of educator wellness. Notice you can self-rate from 1.0–4.0 in increments of 0.5. As you check in on your weekly progress, be sure to indicate the date of your progress check-in so you can observe your progress over time.

Consider sharing your results in figures B.7 and B.8 with a trusted colleague or team. Perhaps establish a team wellness goal in addition to your own wellness goals.

Physical Wellness Dimension

Directions: Complete your *physical wellness* dimension self-rating. If your response to the prompt is yes, check the box. Then rank yourself 1–4 for each routine (consider your number of yes responses), followed by identifying your strengths and routines for possible improvement.

Food routines: Consider what and when you eat and drink, and how well you hydrate during the day.	**Movement routines:** Consider what, when, and how well you move during the day.	**Sleep routines:** Consider how much sleep and rest you get during each twenty-four-hour cycle.
☐ I monitor my food choices most days. ☐ My food choices energize me. ☐ I stay hydrated throughout the day. ☐ I take time to eat breakfast and lunch during my workday. ☐ I am able to eat without distractions. ☐ I monitor how my food choices impact my mood.	☐ I monitor how much I sit or stand each day. ☐ I monitor my number of steps during the day. ☐ I monitor how my movement impacts my mood. ☐ I feel energized most days. ☐ I take brain breaks during my day (perhaps with students). ☐ I practice movement routines with my colleagues or students.	☐ I monitor the hourly amount of my daily sleep. ☐ I feel rested most days when at work. ☐ My sleep positively impacts my mood and behavior. ☐ I use a common daily sleep routine. ☐ I take time to rest during the day without guilt. ☐ I support students or colleagues who may not be getting enough sleep.
1 2 3 4	1 2 3 4	1 2 3 4

Self-Rating: 1 = Beginning; 2 = Implementing; 3 = Embracing; 4 = Modeling

Self-Reflection Plan Of these three physical wellness routines:

Which routine is your greatest strength, and why?	Which routine most needs your attention, and why?

Figure B.1: Educator wellness self-rating and reflection—Physical wellness routines.

Visit **go.SolutionTree.com/educatorwellness** for a free reproducible version of this figure.

Mental Wellness Dimension

Directions: Complete your *mental wellness* dimension self-rating. If your response to the prompt is yes, check the box. Then rank yourself 1–4 for each routine (consider your number of yes responses), followed by identifying your strengths and routines for possible improvement.

Decision routines: Consider how well you reduce, automate, and regulate the decisions you make each day to avoid decision fatigue.				Balance routines: Consider how well you live a busy, high-energy, well-balanced day-to-day work life and avoid prolonged stress.				Efficacy routines: Consider how well you build your confidence and competence and improve your work-life capabilities each day.			
☐ I know the number of educational decisions I make each day. ☐ I automate when and how I do certain work-related tasks. ☐ I avoid being exhausted from the volume of my daily decisions. ☐ I excel at time management. ☐ I know what self-compassion is and practice it. ☐ I self-regulate the positive or negative impact of my decisions on others.				☐ I stay busy without becoming hurried or exhausted. ☐ I fully engage in a high-positive-energy work life each day. ☐ I avoid cynical or negative behaviors. ☐ I commit time for silence and quiet from the daily noise of life. ☐ I maintain positive low-energy time for self-reflection and improvement. ☐ I demonstrate a high-energy, well-balanced professional and joyful life for others to observe.				☐ I know how to improve my self-efficacy. ☐ I practice specific routines to overcome the adversity I encounter each week. ☐ I reframe my doubts into challenges and as opportunities for my growth. ☐ I am confident in my ability to help every child learn. ☐ I continuously seek to improve my competency and knowledge. ☐ I seek evidence of student success as one measure toward my self-efficacy.			
1	2	3	4	1	2	3	4	1	2	3	4

Self-Rating: 1 = Beginning; 2 = Implementing; 3 = Embracing; 4 = Modeling

Self-Reflection Plan Of these three mental wellness routines:

Which routine is your greatest strength, and why?	Which routine most needs your attention, and why?

Figure B.2: Educator wellness self-rating and reflection—Mental wellness routines.

Visit **go.SolutionTree.com/educatorwellness** for a free reproducible version of this figure.

Emotional Wellness Dimension

Directions: Complete your *emotional wellness* dimension self-rating. If your response to the prompt is yes, check the box. Then rank yourself 1–4 for each routine (consider your number of yes responses), followed by identifying your strengths and routines for possible improvement.

Awareness routines: Consider how well you identify, keep track of, and respond to your daily emotions.

- ☐ I pay attention to my emotions each day.
- ☐ I respond positively to my strong, unpleasant emotions like sadness or anger.
- ☐ I share my strong, pleasant emotions like happiness and tenderness with others.
- ☐ I know my negative emotional reactions impact student cognition.
- ☐ I am aware of how my emotional responses impact my colleagues.
- ☐ I collect data on my emotional responses to events and to other people.

1	2	3	4

Understanding routines: Consider the why behind your emotions and how well you reflect on your responses to different emotions.

- ☐ I connect my emotional state to my work-life events and experiences.
- ☐ I know the emotional triggers for my more unpleasant emotions.
- ☐ I take the time to identify patterns related to my daily emotions.
- ☐ I recognize how different emotions can show up in my body.
- ☐ I generally respond positively to others when unpleasant emotions surface.
- ☐ I model healthy emotional responses for students and colleagues.

1	2	3	4

Mindfulness routines: Consider how well you use mindfulness practices to respond rather than react to your strong and more unpleasant emotions.

- ☐ I use available strategies to effectively respond to my strong emotions.
- ☐ I thoughtfully respond more than I negatively react to my daily emotions.
- ☐ I thoughtfully respond more than I negatively react to others' emotions.
- ☐ I engage in daily mindful breathing, meditation, or journaling practices.
- ☐ I model a daily positive emotional response toward students and colleagues.
- ☐ I take time to reflect daily on my emotional impact on others.

1	2	3	4

Self-Rating: 1 = Beginning; 2 = Implementing; 3 = Embracing; 4 = Modeling

Self-Reflection Plan Of these three emotional wellness routines:

Which routine is your greatest strength, and why?	Which routine most needs your attention, and why?

Figure B.3: Educator wellness self-rating and reflection—Emotional wellness routines.

Visit **go.SolutionTree.com/educatorwellness** for a free reproducible version of this figure.

Social Wellness Dimension

Directions: Complete your *social wellness* dimension self-rating. If your response to the prompt is yes, check the box. Then rank yourself 1-4 for each routine (consider your number of yes responses), followed by identifying your strengths and routines for possible improvement.

Relationship routines: Consider how well you and your colleagues build strong relationships and social connections together.	**Trust routines:** Consider how well you build daily work-life routines of vulnerability and deep listening without judgment of others.	**Purpose routines:** Consider how your daily work life feeds into your greater purpose and helps you find meaning and joy in your work life.
☐ I know my well-being is connected to my daily effort to enhance the lives of others. ☐ I know close positive relationships are a predictor of success in life. ☐ I initiate strong, positive relationships with colleagues. ☐ I work with colleagues and students to create cultural norms of belonging and inclusion. ☐ I work with my colleagues to improve my communication skills. ☐ I seek to build a social support network of colleagues and friends.	☐ I have colleagues I trust. ☐ I practice deep listening without judgment of others. ☐ I am able to be vulnerable with colleagues by asking for help. ☐ I practice vulnerability with my colleagues in order to build trust. ☐ I have colleagues and friends I often seek for help, wisdom, or advice. ☐ I actively seek to model and build trust with students and colleagues.	☐ My career is my vocation—part of something bigger than myself. ☐ My role as an educator is something I feel compelled to do with my life, no matter the challenges. ☐ My role as an educator connects me to my greater purpose. ☐ I know and understand the contributions I am making toward the growth of others. ☐ I know my improvement in physical, mental, and emotional routines impacts my overall social wellness and purpose.
1 2 3 4	1 2 3 4	1 2 3 4

Self-Rating: 1 = Beginning; 2 = Implementing; 3 = Embracing; 4 = Modeling

Self-Reflection Plan Of these three social wellness routines:

Which routine is your greatest strength, and why?	Which routine most needs your attention, and why?

Figure B.4: Educator wellness self-rating and reflection—Social wellness routines.

Visit **go.SolutionTree.com/educatorwellness** for a free reproducible version of this figure.

Educator Wellness Planning Tool—Strengths

Directions: Based on your self-rating responses from figures B.1–B.4 (pages 84–87), identify the routines that are currently strengths for you here, in figure B.5. In the space provided, write one strategy that works for you. Start it with the phrase *I do* . . . .

***Physical* Wellness**	Food Routine Strategies	Movement Routine Strategies	Sleep Routine Strategies
***Mental* Wellness**	Decision Routine Strategies	Balance Routine Strategies	Efficacy Routine Strategies
***Emotional* Wellness**	Awareness Routine Strategies	Understanding Routine Strategies	Mindfulness Routine Strategies
***Social* Wellness**	Relationship Routine Strategies	Trust Routine Strategies	Purpose Routine Strategies

Figure B.5: Educator wellness planning tool—*Routines that are strengths.*

Visit **go.SolutionTree.com/educatorwellness** for a free reproducible version of this figure.

Educator Wellness Planning Tool—Routines for Improvement

Directions: Based on your self-rating responses from figures B.1–B.4 (pages 84–87), identify the routines that are currently in need of improvement for you here, in figure B.6. In the space provided, write one action to get started. Lead with the phrase *I will . . . .*

Physical **Wellness**	Food Routine Strategies	Movement Routine Strategies	Sleep Routine Strategies
Mental **Wellness**	Decision Routine Strategies	Balance Routine Strategies	Efficacy Routine Strategies
Emotional **Wellness**	Awareness Routine Strategies	Understanding Routine Strategies	Mindfulness Routine Strategies
Social **Wellness**	Relationship Routine Strategies	Trust Routine Strategies	Purpose Routine Strategies

Figure B.6: Educator wellness planning tool—*Routines for improvement.*

Visit **go.SolutionTree.com/educatorwellness** for a free reproducible version of this figure.

Educator Wellness Goal Setting, Planning, and Progress Monitoring

Directions: Based on your self-rating and planning responses from figures B.1–B.6 (pages 84–89), identify *physical and mental* wellness routines to measure your progress and proficiency. Be sure to indicate the date for each progress check. Fill in or X the boxes.

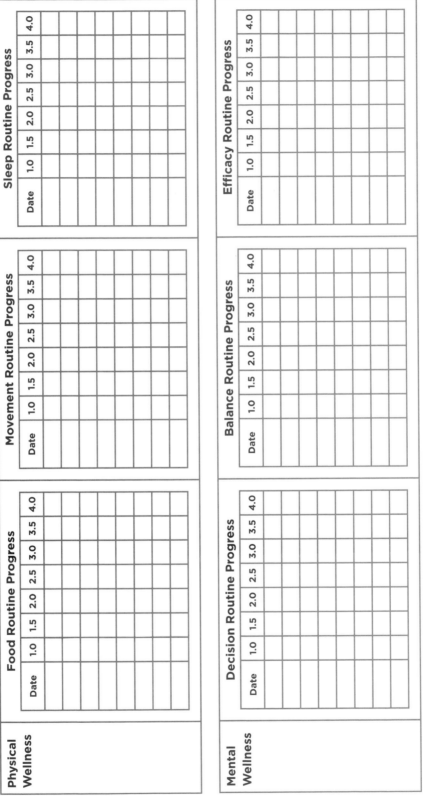

Figure B.7: Educator wellness goal setting and planning tool—*Physical and mental wellness progress monitoring.*

Visit **go.SolutionTree.com/educatorwellness** for a free reproducible version of this figure.

Educator Wellness Goal Setting, Planning, and Progress Monitoring

Directions: Based on your self-rating and planning responses from figures B.1–B.6 (pages 84–89), identify *emotional and social wellness* routines to measure your progress and proficiency. Be sure to indicate the date for each progress check. Fill in or X the boxes.

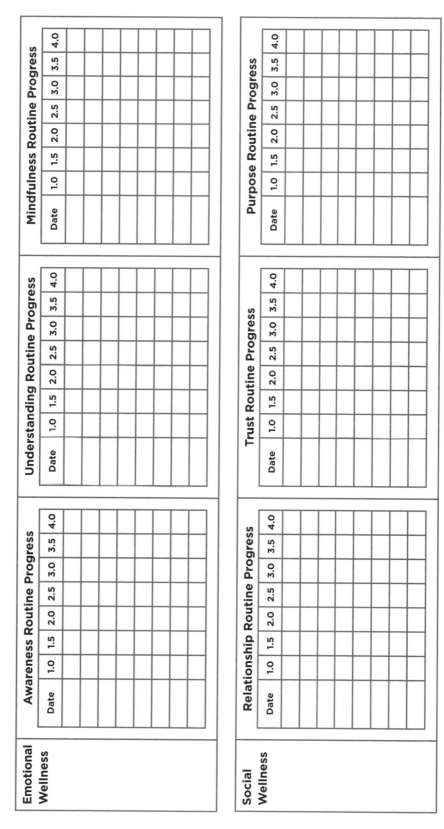

Figure B.8: Educator wellness goal setting and planning tool—*Emotional and social wellness progress monitoring.*

Visit **go.SolutionTree.com/educatorwellness** for a free reproducible version of this figure.

Wellness Solutions for Educators *Self-Evaluation Rubric*

Directions: Rate your proficiency in each of the four dimensions in figure C.1.

Four Educator Wellness Dimensions	Description of Level 1	Does not meet	Shows limited fulfillment	Substantially meets	Fully achieves	Description of Level 4
Physical Wellness Dimension Food Movement Sleep	I struggle to take care of my food, sleep, and movement routines. I do not sleep well and often feel sluggish. I do not monitor or take action to improve my physical wellness.	1	2	3	4	My physical wellness routines are a priority in my life. I daily pay attention to and monitor my healthy habits in relation to my food, sleep, and movement routines. I feel great physically and am energized and well rested most days. I am able to take time for my own physical wellness and encourage others to do so as well.
Mental Wellness Dimension Decision Balance Efficacy	I feel overwhelmed by the number of decisions I need to make each day. I feel exhausted. I feel hurried and behind most days. It is difficult for me to place boundaries on the demands for my time and find positive low-energy time to reflect and renew. I often lack confidence in my ability to do my job.	1	2	3	4	I feel a strong sense of confidence in my life. I work hard to balance quiet, reflective time against the demands of my work life. I am busy and lead a thriving, full life. I automate, regulate, and reduce many routines and expectations for my daily decision making, and most of my decisions are a result of thoughtful reflection and planning. I bring a high-positive-energy state each day and actively seek evidence of my competence.
Emotional Wellness Dimension Awareness Understanding Mindfulness	I am detached from my emotions or consumed by them. I often feel as if my emotions are controlling me, and I react impulsively to them. I do not know how to respond to my strong emotions without upsetting colleagues, students, myself, or others. I do not use any reflection strategies in order to respond to my emotions more thoughtfully.	1	2	3	4	I am aware of my daily emotions. I am able to build an understanding of and recognize the sources of my emotional responses. I utilize mindfulness practices to better understand the why behind my emotions and experiences, and to better engage in healthy responses to my strong and sometimes more unpleasant emotions.
Social Wellness Dimension Relationship Trust Purpose	I often feel as if I don't belong and have a hard time connecting to others. I rarely ask for help. I view asking for help as a weakness and not a strength of mine. I have a difficult time trusting my colleagues and team members and generally prefer to do my work alone. My job does not provide much meaning for me.	1	2	3	4	I have strong, positive relationships with my colleagues. I practice active listening skills and work hard to improve all of my work- and home-life relationships every day. I am confident enough in my abilities to know when to ask for help and become more vulnerable with others. I help my colleagues feel connected and build trusting relationships. I embrace my responsibility to contribute to the greater good of my profession. My job provides meaning and fulfillment to my life.

Figure C.1: Wellness Solutions for Educators *self-evaluation rubric.*

Visit **go.SolutionTree.com/educatorwellness** for a free reproducible version of this figure.

Notes

Introduction

1   Burke, A. E., & Hicks, P. J. (n.d.). *Chapter 4: Wellness and its impact on professionalism.* Accessed at www.abp.org/professionalism-guide/chapter-4/wellness on April 17, 2021.

Chapter 1

2   Rath, T. (2013). *Eat move sleep: How small choices lead to big changes.* Arlington, VA: Missionday.

3   Leibman, P. (n.d.). *The four energy zones (Your energy level is not just high or low).* Accessed at https://strongerhabits.com/energy-quadrant on July 8, 2021.

4   Greer, S. M., Goldstein, A. N., & Walker, M. P. (2013). *The impact of sleep deprivation on food desire in the human brain.* Accessed at www.nature.com/articles/ncomms3259?utm_medium=affiliate&utm_source=commission_junction&utm_campaign=3_nsn6445_deeplink_PID100064639&utm_content=deeplink on April 19, 2021.

5   Newsom, R. (2020). *Diet and exercise and sleep.* Accessed at www.sleepfoundation.org/physical-health/diet-exercise-sleep on June 23, 2021.

6   Centers for Disease Control and Prevention. (2021). *Healthy eating for a healthy weight.* Accessed at www.cdc.gov/healthyweight/healthy_eating/index.html on July 8, 2021.

7   Greer, S. M., Goldstein, A. N., & Walker, M. P. (2013). *The impact of sleep deprivation on food desire in the human brain.* Accessed at www.nature.com/articles/ncomms3259?utm_medium=affiliate&utm_source=commission_junction&utm_campaign=3_nsn6445_deeplink_PID100064639&utm_content=deeplink on April 19, 2021.

8   Crichton-Stuart, C. (2020). *What are the benefits of eating healthy?* Accessed at www.medicalnewstoday.com/articles/322268 on April 19, 2021.

9   Rath, T. (2013). *Eat move sleep: How small choices lead to big changes.* Arlington, VA: Missionday.

10   Fox, N. (2019). *The many health risks of processed foods.* Accessed at www.lhsfna.org/index.cfm/lifelines/may-2019/the-many-health-risks-of-processed-foods on April 19, 2021.

11	Olivares, L. (2018). *Tidbits from trainings: How to know you're well hydrated.* Accessed at https://aghealth.ucdavis.edu/news/how-know-youre-well-hydrated-tidbits-our-trainings on June 23, 2021.

12	Centers for Disease Control and Prevention. (2021). *3 reasons to work out with a friend.* Accessed at www.cdc.gov/diabetes/library/spotlights/workout-buddy.html on July 8, 2021.

13	Gupta, S. (2020). *Keep sharp: Build a better brain at any age.* New York: Simon & Schuster.

14	Ibid.

15	Langshur, E., & Klemp, N. (2016). *Start here: Master the lifelong habit of wellbeing.* New York: Gallery Books.

16	McGonigal, K. (2019). *The joy of movement: How exercise helps us find happiness, hope, connection, and courage.* New York: Avery.

17	Rath, T. (2013). *Eat move sleep: How small choices lead to big changes.* Arlington, VA: Missionday.

18	McGonigal, K. (2019). *The joy of movement: How exercise helps us find happiness, hope, connection, and courage.* New York: Avery.

19	National Institute on Aging. (2021). *Four types of exercise can improve your health and physical ability.* Accessed at www.nia.nih.gov/health/four-types-exercise-can-improve-your-health-and-physical-ability on June 23, 2021.

20	Rath, T. (2013). *Eat move sleep: How small choices lead to big changes.* Arlington, VA: Missionday.

21	Raupers, E. (2018). *Physical wellness: What it is, why it's important, and how to cultivate it.* Accessed at https://sites.psu.edu/healthypennstate/2018/02/26/physical-wellness-what-it-is-why-its-important-and-how-to-cultivate-it/#:~:text=If%20you%20are%20sleep-deprived%2C%20your%20memory%20will%20not,as%20well.%20How%20do%20you%20cultivate%20Physical%20Wellness%3F on April 23, 2021.

22	National Heart, Lung, and Blood Institute. (n.d.). *Sleep deprivation and deficiency.* Accessed at www.nhlbi.nih.gov/health-topics/sleep-deprivation-and-deficiency on April 19, 2021.

23	Gupta, S. (2020). *Keep sharp: Build a better brain at any age.* New York: Simon & Schuster, p. 136.

24	Newsom, R. (2020). *Diet and exercise and sleep.* Accessed at www.sleepfoundation.org/physical-health/diet-exercise-sleep on June 29, 2021.

25	Rath, T. (2013). *Eat move sleep: How small choices lead to big changes.* Arlington, VA: Missionday, p. 140.

26	Rath, T. (2013). *Eat move sleep: How small choices lead to big changes.* Arlington, VA: Missionday, p. 19.

27	Fleming, S. (2019). *This is how companies in Japan are fighting the country's sleeplessness epidemic.* Accessed at www.weforum.org/agenda/2019/01/this-is-how-companies-in-japan-are-fighting-sleeplessness-epidemic on June 23, 2021.

28	Ibid.

29	Ibid.

30 Jabr, F. (2016). *Q&A: Why a rested brain is more creative.* Accessed at www.scientificamerican
    .com/article/q-a-why-a-rested-brain-is-more-creative on June 23, 2021.

31 Kanold, T. D. (2017). *HEART! Fully forming your professional life as a teacher and leader.*
    Bloomington, IN: Solution Tree Press.

32 Clear, J. (2018). *Atomic habits: An easy and proven way to build good habits and break bad ones.*
    New York: Avery.

Chapter 2

33 World Health Organization. (2018). *Mental health: Strengthening our response.* Accessed at
    www.who.int/news-room/fact-sheets/detail/mental-health-strengthening-our-response on
    July 6, 2021.

34 ULifeline. (n.d.). *How do you tell the difference between good stress and bad?* Accessed at
    www.ulifeline.org/articles/450-good-stress-bad-stress on April 14, 2021.

35 Ibid.

36 World Health Organization. (2019). *Burn-out an "occupational phenomenon": International
    classification of diseases.* Accessed at www.who.int/news/item/28-05-2019-burn-out-an
    -occupational-phenomenon-international-classification-of-diseases on July 6, 2021.

37 Mental Health Foundation. (n.d.). *How to support mental health at work.* Accessed at www
    .mentalhealth.org.uk/publications/how-support-mental-health-work on March 16, 2021.

38 Lamothe, C. (2019). *Understanding decision fatigue.* Accessed at www.healthline.com/health
    /decision-fatigue on March 19, 2021.

39 Goldberg, G., & Houser, R. (2017, July 19). *Battling decision fatigue* [Blog post]. Accessed
    at www.edutopia.org/blog/battling-decision-fatigue-gravity-goldberg-renee-houser on
    April 19, 2021.

40 Tierney, J. (2011). *Do you suffer from decision fatigue?* Accessed at www.nytimes.
    com/2011/08/21/magazine/do-you-suffer-from-decision-fatigue.html on June 23, 2021.

41 Boogren, T. H. (2021). *Coaching for educator wellness: A guide to supporting new and experienced
    teachers.* Bloomington, IN: Solution Tree Press.

42 Neff, K., & Germer, C. (2017). Self-compassion and psychological well-being. In E. M.
    Seppälä, E. Simon-Thomas, S. L. Brown, M. C. Worline, C. D. Cameron, & J. R. Doty
    (Eds.), *The Oxford handbook of compassion science* (pp. 371–386). New York: Oxford University
    Press, p. 371.

43 Germer, C., & Neff, K. (2013). Self-compassion in clinical practice. *Journal of Clinical
    Psychology, 69*(8), 856–867, p. 857.

44 Turkle, S. (2012, February). *Connected, but alone?* [Video file]. Accessed at www.ted.com/talks
    /sherry_turkle_connected_but_alone/transcript on July 20, 2020.

45 Holiday, R. (2019). *Stillness is the key.* New York: Portfolio/Penguin, p. 215.

46 Bandura, A. (1977). Self-efficacy: Toward a unifying theory of behavioral change. *Psychological
    Review, 84*(2), 191–215.

47 Pfeffer, J., & Sutton, R. I. (2006). *Hard facts, dangerous half-truths, and total nonsense: Profiting
    from evidence-based management.* Boston: Harvard Business School Press, p. 52.

48   Kross, E. (2021). *Chatter: The voice in our head, why it matters, and how to harness it.* New York: Crown, p. xix.

49   Ibid.

50   Bandura, A. (1997). *Self-efficacy: The exercise of control.* New York: W.H. Freeman and Company.

51   Bandura, A. (2012). *On the functional properties of perceived self-efficacy revisited.* Accessed at https://journals.sagepub.com/doi/full/10.1177/0149206311410606 on June 23, 2021.

52   Gupta, S. (2020). *Keep sharp: Build a better brain at any age.* New York: Simon & Schuster.

53   Kross, E. (2021). *Chatter: The voice in our head, why it matters, and how to harness it.* New York: Crown.

Chapter 3

54   Emotion. (n.d.). In *Merriam-Webster's online dictionary.* Accessed at www.merriam-webster.com/dictionary/emotion on April 16, 2021.

55   Brackett, M. A., & Simmons, D. (2015). Emotions matter. *Educational Leadership, 73*(2), 22–27.

56   Institute for Health and Human Potential. (n.d.). *The meaning of emotional intelligence.* Accessed at www.ihhp.com/meaning-of-emotional-intelligence on July 7, 2021.

57   Goleman, D. (1995). *Emotional intelligence: Why it can matter more than IQ.* New York: Bantam Books.

58   Institute for Health and Human Potential. (n.d.). *The meaning of emotional intelligence.* Accessed at www.ihhp.com/meaning-of-emotional-intelligence on July 7, 2021

59   Yale Center for Emotional Intelligence. (n.d.). *What we do.* Accessed at www.ycei.org/what-we-do on April 19, 2021.

60   Marzano, R. J., & Marzano, J. S. (2015). *Managing the inner world of teaching: Emotions, interpretations, and actions.* Bloomington, IN: Marzano Resources, p. 2.

61   Tomlinson, C. A., & Sousa, D. A. (2020). *The sciences of teaching.* Accessed at www.ascd.org/publications/educational-leadership/may20/vol77/num08/The-Sciences-of-Teaching.aspx on April 22, 2021.

62   Chiao, J. Y. (2017). Cultural neuroscience of compassion and empathy. In E. M. Seppälä, E. Simon-Thomas, S. L. Brown, M. C. Worline, C. D. Cameron, & J. R. Doty (Eds.), *The Oxford handbook of compassion science* (pp. 147–158). New York: Oxford University Press, p. 153.

63   Niemi, K. (2020). *CASEL is updating the most widely recognized definition of social-emotional learning. Here's why.* Accessed at www.the74million.org/article/niemi-casel-is-updating-the-most-widely-recognized-definition-of-social-emotional-learning-heres-why on July 7, 2021.

64   Brackett, M. (2019). *Permission to feel: Unlocking the power of emotions to help our kids, ourselves, and our society thrive.* New York: Celadon Books, p. 23.

65   Brown, B. (n.d.). *Downloads.* Accessed at https://brenebrown.com/downloads on April 19, 2021.

66 Brackett, M. (2019). *Permission to feel: Unlocking the power of emotions to help our kids, ourselves, and our society thrive.* New York: Celadon Books.

67 Ibid.

68 David, S. (2016). *Emotional agility: Get unstuck, embrace change, and thrive in work and life.* New York: Avery.

69 Pennebaker, J. W. (1997). Writing about emotional experiences as a therapeutic process. *Psychological Science, 8*(3), 162–166.

70 David, S. (2016). *You can write your way out of an emotional funk. Here's how.* Accessed at www .thecut.com/2016/09/journaling-can-help-you-out-of-a-bad-mood.html on April 19, 2021.

71 Kabat-Zinn, J. (2003). Mindfulness-based interventions in context: Past, present, and future. *Clinical Psychology: Science and Practice, 10*(2), 144–156, p. 145.

72 Greater Good in Action. (n.d.). *Mindful breathing.* Accessed at https://ggia.berkeley.edu /practice/mindful_breathing on April 19, 2021.

73 Alderman, L. (2016). *Breathe. Exhale. Repeat: The benefits of controlled breathing.* Accessed at www.nytimes.com/2016/11/09/well/mind/breathe-exhale-repeat-the-benefits-of-controlled -breathing.html on July 8, 2021.

74 Headspace. (n.d.). *What is meditation?* Accessed at www.headspace.com/meditation-101/what -is-meditation on April 19, 2021.

75 Pennebaker, J. W. (1997). Writing about emotional experiences as a therapeutic process. *Psychological Science, 8*(3), 162–166.

76 Tucker, A. (2020). *How to start a mindful journaling practice.* Accessed at www.mindful.org /how-to-start-a-mindful-journaling-practice on April 19, 2021.

77 Nortje, A. (2021). *Journaling for mindfulness: 44 prompts, examples, and exercises.* Accessed at https://positivepsychology.com/journaling-for-mindfulness on April 19, 2021.

78 Mason, C., Rivers Murphy, M. M., & Jackson, Y. (2019). *Mindfulness practices: Cultivating heart centered communities where students focus and flourish.* Bloomington, IN: Solution Tree Press.

79 Carlson, D. E. (1988). *Counseling and self-esteem.* Waco, TX: World Books.

Chapter 4

80 Benkler, Y. (2011). The unselfish gene. *Harvard Business Review, 89*(7–8), 76–85, p. 77.

81 Goleman, D. (2006). *Social intelligence: The new science of human relationships.* New York: Bantam Books, p.1.

82 Ibid.

83 Gupta, S. (2020). *Keep sharp: Build a better brain at any age.* New York: Simon & Schuster, p. 191.

84 Mineo, L. (2017). *Good genes are nice, but joy is better.* Accessed at https://news.harvard.edu /gazette/story/2017/04/over-nearly-80-years-harvard-study-has-been-showing-how-to-live-a -healthy-and-happy-life on July 2, 2020.

85 Heller, R. (2020). Organizing schools so teachers can succeed: A conversation with Susan Moore Johnson. *Phi Delta Kappan, 101*(6), 35–39, p. 35.

86 Ibid.

87 Visible Learning. (n.d.). *Hattie ranking: 252 influences and effect sizes related to student achievement.* Accessed at https://visible-learning.org/hattie-ranking-influences-effect-sizes -learning-achievement on July 9, 2021.

88 Rath, T. (2020). *Life's great question: Discover how you contribute to the world.* San Francisco: Silicon Guild Books, p. 12.

89 Reeves, D. B. (2006). *The learning leader: How to focus school improvement for better results.* Alexandria, VA: Association for Supervision and Curriculum Development.

90 Kanold, T. D. (2011). *The five disciplines of PLC leaders.* Bloomington, IN: Solution Tree Press, p. 85.

91 Reeves, D. B. (2006). *The learning leader: How to focus school improvement for better results.* Alexandria, VA: Association for Supervision and Curriculum Development.

92 Seppälä, E. (2017). *Turns out burnout is linked to loneliness—Here's what you can do about it.* Accessed at https://emmaseppala.com/burnout-at-work-isnt-just-about-exhaustion-its-also -about-loneliness on April 19, 2021.

93 Ibid.

94 Zak, P. J. (2017). *The neuroscience of trust.* Accessed at https://hbr.org/2017/01/the -neuroscience-of-trust on July 2, 2020.

95 Trust. (n.d.). In *Merriam-Webster's online dictionary.* Accessed at www.merriam-webster.com /dictionary/trust on April 19, 2021.

96 Brown, B. (2012). *Daring greatly: How the courage to be vulnerable transforms the way we live, love, parent, and lead.* New York: Gotham Books, p. 10.

97 Zak, P. J. (2017). *The neuroscience of trust.* Accessed at https://hbr.org/2017/01/the -neuroscience-of-trust on June 26, 2021.

98 Ibid.

99 Coyle, D. (2018). *The culture code: The secrets of highly successful groups.* New York: Bantam Books, p. 103.

100 Ibid.

101 Reis, H. T., Crasta, D., Rogge, R. D., Maniaci, M. R., & Carmichael, C. L. (2018). *Perceived Partner Responsiveness Scale.* Accessed at www.sas.rochester.edu/psy/people/faculty/reis_harry /assets/pdf/reisetal_2018_pprs.pdf on June 24, 2021.

102 King, M. (2021). *Social chemistry: Decoding the patterns of human connection.* New York: Dutton.

103 Ibid, p. 205.

104 Ibid, p. 205.

105 Ibid, p. 206.

106 Gallup. (2017). *Gallup Daily: U.S. employee engagement.* Accessed at www.gallup.com/poll /180404/gallup-daily-employee-engagement.aspx on June 23, 2021.

107 Palmer, P. J. (2000). *Let your life speak: Listening for the voice of vocation.* San Francisco: Jossey-Bass, pp. 4–5.

108 Brooks, D. (2019). *The second mountain: The quest for a moral life.* New York: Random House, p. 91.

109 BlackPast. (2012). *(1896) Booker T. Washington, "Address to the Harvard Alumni Dinner".* Accessed at www.blackpast.org/african-american-history/1896-booker-t-washington-address -harvard-alumni-dinner on April 19, 2021.

110 Washington Post Live. (2021). *Transcript: Be well: The value of self-care.* Accessed at www .washingtonpost.com/washington-post-live/2021/03/18/transcript-be-well-value-self-care on April 19, 2021.

111 Ibid.

112 BlackPast. (2012). *(1896) Booker T. Washington, "Address to the Harvard Alumni Dinner".* Accessed at www.blackpast.org/african-american-history/1896-booker-t-washington-address- harvard-alumni-dinner on April 19, 2021.

Index

HEART!
Timothy D. Kanold
Explore the concept of a heartprint—the distinctive impression an educator's heart leaves on students and colleagues during his or her professional career. Use this resource to reflect on your professional journey, discover how to increase efficacy, and foster productive, heart-centered classrooms and schools.
BKF749

SOUL!
Timothy D. Kanold
Chart a deeply rewarding journey toward discovering your soul story—the pursuit of your moral good, to create good in others. Refreshing and uplifting, this resource includes dozens of real stories from educators, as well as ample space for journaling and self-reflection.
BKF982

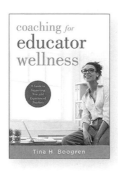

Coaching for Educator Wellness
Tina H. Boogren
Acquire evergreen coaching strategies alongside fresh new solutions for differentiating support for new and veteran teachers, addressing teacher self-care, and more. You'll turn to this resource again and again as you continue to improve your craft and help teachers find their own greatness.
BKF989

180 Days of Self-Care for Busy Educators
Tina H. Boogren
Rely on *180 Days of Self-Care for Busy Educators* to help you lead a happier, healthier, more fulfilled life inside and outside of the classroom. With Tina H. Boogren's guidance, you will work through thirty six weeks of self-care strategies during the school year.
BKF920

GL BAL PD

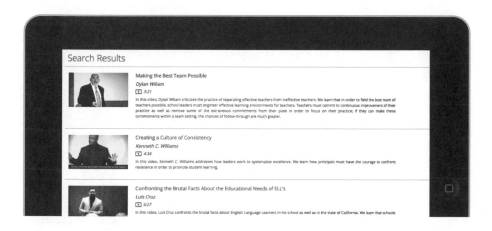

Access **Hundreds of Videos & Books** from Top Experts

Global PD gives educators focused and goals-oriented training from top experts. You can rely on this innovative online tool to improve instruction in every classroom.

- Gain job-embedded PD from the largest library of PLC videos and books in the world.

- Customize learning based on skill level and time commitments; videos are less than 20 minutes, and books can be browsed by chapter to accommodate busy schedules.

- Get unlimited, on-demand access—24 hours a day.

▶ **LEARN MORE**
SolutionTree.com/GlobalPDLibrary

 Solution Tree